THE
ELDERLY
OPPOSING VIEWPOINTS®

Other Books of Related Interest in the Opposing Viewpoints Series:

America's Future
Biomedical Ethics
Death and Dying
Economics in America
Euthanasia
The Health Crisis
The Homeless
Poverty
Social Justice

Additional Books in the Opposing Viewpoints Series:

Abortion
AIDS
American Foreign Policy
American Government
American Values
America's Elections
America's Prisons
Animal Rights
Censorship
Central America
Chemical Dependency
China
Civil Liberties
Constructing a Life Philosophy
Crime and Criminals
Criminal Justice
The Death Penalty
Drug Abuse
The Environmental Crisis
Genetic Engineering
Israel
Japan
Latin America and U.S. Foreign Policy
Male/Female Roles
The Mass Media
The Middle East
Nuclear War
The Political Spectrum
Problems of Africa
Religion in America
Science & Religion
Sexual Values
The Soviet Union
The Superpowers: A New Detente
Teenage Sexuality
Terrorism
The Third World
The Vietnam War
Violence in America
War and Human Nature

THE ELDERLY

OPPOSING VIEWPOINTS®

David L. Bender & Bruno Leone, *Series Editors*

Karin Swisher, *Book Editor*
Tara P. Deal, *Assistant Editor*

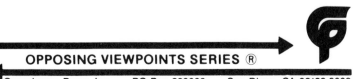

OPPOSING VIEWPOINTS SERIES ®

Greenhaven Press, Inc.   PO Box 289009   San Diego, CA 92128-9009

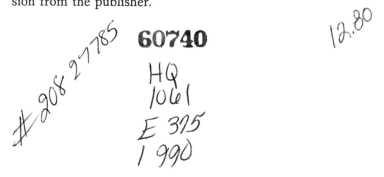

Library of Congress Cataloging-in-Publication Data

The Elderly : opposing viewpoints / Karin Swisher, book editor, Tara P. Deal, assistant editor.
    p.   cm. — (Opposing viewpoints series)
    Includes bibliographical references.
    Summary: Various authors debate age-related issues: How does society view the elderly? Do the elderly need outside help? Is social security distributed fairly? and Can society meet the elderly's health care needs?
    ISBN 0-89908-475-3 (lib. bdg.). — ISBN 0-89908-450-8 (pbk.)
    1. Aged. 2. Aged—Care. 3. Aged—Health and hygiene. 4. Social Security. [1. Aged. 2. Critical thinking.] I. Swisher. Karin, 1966-   . II. Deal, Tara P., 1965-   . III. Series.
HQ1061.E375   1990
305.26—dc20
                                                        89-25950
                                                            CIP
                                                             AC

"Congress shall make no law . . .
abridging the freedom of speech,
or of the press."

First Amendment to the US Constitution

The basic foundation of our democracy is the first amendment
guarantee of freedom of expression. The *Opposing Viewpoints
Series* is dedicated to the concept of this basic freedom and the
idea that it is more important to practice it than to enshrine it.

Contents

Why Consider Opposing Viewpoints?

"It is better to debate a question without settling it than to settle a question without debating it."

Joseph Joubert (1754-1824)

The Importance of Examining Opposing Viewpoints

The purpose of the Opposing Viewpoints Series, and this book in particular, is to present balanced, and often difficult to find, opposing points of view on complex and sensitive issues.

Probably the best way to become informed is to analyze the positions of those who are regarded as experts and well studied on issues. It is important to consider every variety of opinion in an attempt to determine the truth. Opinions from the mainstream of society should be examined. But also important are opinions that are considered radical, reactionary, or minority as well as those stigmatized by some other uncomplimentary label. An important lesson of history is the eventual acceptance of many unpopular and even despised opinions. The ideas of Socrates, Jesus, and Galileo are good examples of this.

Readers will approach this book with their own opinions on the issues debated within it. However, to have a good grasp of one's own viewpoint, it is necessary to understand the arguments of those with whom one disagrees. It can be said that those who do not completely understand their adversary's point of view do not fully understand their own.

A persuasive case for considering opposing viewpoints has been presented by John Stuart Mill in his work *On Liberty*. When examining controversial issues it may be helpful to reflect on this suggestion:

> The only way in which a human being can make some approach to knowing the whole of a subject, is by hearing what can be said about it by persons of every variety of opinion, and studying all modes in which it can be looked at by every character of mind. No wise man ever acquired his wisdom in any mode but this.

Analyzing Sources of Information

The Opposing Viewpoints Series includes diverse materials taken from magazines, journals, books, and newspapers, as well as statements and position papers from a wide range of individuals, organizations and governments. This broad spectrum of sources helps to develop patterns of thinking which are open to the consideration of a variety of opinions.

Pitfalls to Avoid

A pitfall to avoid in considering opposing points of view is that of regarding one's own opinion as being common sense and the most rational stance and the point of view of others as being only opinion and naturally wrong. It may be that another's opinion is correct and one's own is in error.

Another pitfall to avoid is that of closing one's mind to the opinions of those with whom one disagrees. The best way to approach a dialogue is to make one's primary purpose that of understanding the mind and arguments of the other person and not that of enlightening him or her with one's own solutions. More can be learned by listening than speaking.

It is my hope that after reading this book the reader will have a deeper understanding of the issues debated and will appreciate the complexity of even seemingly simple issues on which good and honest people disagree. This awareness is particularly important in a democratic society such as ours where people enter into public debate to determine the common good. Those with whom one disagrees should not necessarily be regarded as enemies, but perhaps simply as people who suggest different paths to a common goal.

Developing Basic Reading and Thinking Skills

In this book, carefully edited opposing viewpoints are purposely placed back to back to create a running debate; each viewpoint is preceded by a short quotation that best expresses the author's main argument. This format instantly plunges the reader into the midst of a controversial issue and greatly aids that reader in mastering the basic skill of recognizing an author's point of view.

A number of basic skills for critical thinking are practiced in the activities that appear throughout the books in the series. Some of the skills are:

Evaluating Sources of Information   The ability to choose from among alternative sources the most reliable and accurate source in relation to a given subject.

Separating Fact from Opinion   The ability to make the basic distinction between factual statements (those that can be demonstrated or verified empirically) and statements of opinion (those that are beliefs or attitudes that cannot be proved).

Identifying Stereotypes   The ability to identify oversimplified, exaggerated descriptions (favorable or unfavorable) about people and insulting statements about racial, religious or national groups, based upon misinformation or lack of information.

Recognizing Ethnocentrism   The ability to recognize attitudes or opinions that express the view that one's own race, culture, or group is inherently superior, or those attitudes that judge another culture or group in terms of one's own.

It is important to consider opposing viewpoints and equally important to be able to critically analyze those viewpoints. The activities in this book are designed to help the reader master these thinking skills. Statements are taken from the book's viewpoints and the reader is asked to analyze them. This technique aids the reader in developing skills that not only can be applied to the viewpoints in this book, but also to situations where opinionated spokespersons comment on controversial issues. Although the activities are helpful to the solitary reader, they are most useful when the reader can benefit from the interaction of group discussion.

Using this book and others in the series should help readers develop basic reading and thinking skills. These skills should improve the reader's ability to understand what they read. Readers should be better able to separate fact from opinion, substance from rhetoric and become better consumers of information in our media-centered culture.

This volume of the Opposing Viewpoints Series does not advocate a particular point of view. Quite the contrary! The very nature of the book leaves it to the reader to formulate the opinions he or she finds most suitable. My purpose as publisher is to see that this is made possible by offering a wide range of viewpoints which are fairly presented.

David L. Bender
Publisher

Introduction

"When we have lived our generation out, we should not wish to encroach upon another."

Thomas Jefferson in a letter to John Adams

The Census Bureau estimates that people over age 65 will constitute 20.7 percent of the U.S. population in 2030 and that life expectancy will most likely increase above today's expected age of 75. These shifting demographics, many argue, are cause for grave concern. The huge baby-boom generation is aging rapidly. This will mean that the children and grandchildren of the baby-boomers—a much smaller generation—must pay for their care. Many fear that this will engender a crisis in equity between the generations, that the young will be forced to take on a burden which they will be unable to bear. It is time, these people argue, to ration our medical technology, Social Security, and Medicare benefits in anticipation of these changes in the age of our population.

Those who support rationing benefits and technology believe it is an economic imperative. Richard D. Lamm, former governor of Colorado, is perhaps the most vocal advocate of this view: "We have to insure that our policies toward the elderly do not impoverish our children, and we must make sure they do not create a burden for coming generations. . . . There is something terribly inappropriate about a society which doesn't even provide basic health care to millions of people and yet amends its Medicare regulations to pay for heart transplants—a number of which go to the wealthy elderly." Lamm and others view medical resources as limited. They believe that society must make a choice between its young and its aged, and that the choice should be made in favor of the young.

In addition, Lamm and others argue that America's obsession with youth and long life aggravates the problem. The elderly should accept the notion of a "natural life span," they believe. Essentially, they recommend that once people reach the age of 70-80, they should voluntarily decide not to have expensive life-saving operations such as organ transplants. Again, they cite the issue of equity. As Lamm says, "I find it morally offensive at the age of even 52 to demand the same level of medical treatment as someone who has their whole life ahead of them."

13

Opponents of this view take a moral stance. They believe that the elderly deserve the same medical and other care as younger generations receive. To do less, these supporters argue, is an insidious form of discrimination. As Ruth Sperber claims in an editorial in *The Nation*, "Let us not, in the rush to cut costs and balance budgets, forget our elderly who helped build this state and nation and who spent a lifetime working and paying taxes."

Others point out that deciding to allocate resources to the old does not mean burdening the young, and limiting resources to the elderly does not necessarily mean others will benefit. In fact, the entire argument seems to be invented to pit the young against the old, these critics say, to distract both groups from the need to increase social programs across the board. As Meredith Minkler, associate professor at the University of California at Berkeley, argues, "The scapegoating of the elderly as a primary cause of the fiscal crisis . . . has been used as a political tool to stoke resentment of the elderly and to create perceptions of a forced competition of the aged and younger members of society for limited resources." Minkler and others believe society must foster a "collective vision" of medical and social services and that we must provide for all poor citizens, from infants to the aged. Ruth Sperber seconds this argument: "To assume that the elderly may use up only that percentage of medical costs that is equal to their percentage of the total population is a misuse of statistics. . . . AIDS is not a disease of the elderly, yet we do not begrudge that expense."

The issue of whether society's resources must be divided is likely to continue. The authors included in *The Elderly: Opposing Viewpoints* examine the current and future state of the elderly in America. Their arguments address these questions: How Does Society View the Elderly? Are the Elderly Poor? Is Social Security Necessary for the Elderly? How Should Society Meet the Elderly's Health Care Needs? As readers explore these issues, they should consider what society's responsibility to the aged should be.

CHAPTER 1

How Does Society View the Elderly?

Chapter Preface

As more people grow old in America, society's views of who the elderly are and what they want are changing. Lynda Hurst, writing in the *Toronto Star* daily newspaper, states, "The graying of the baby-boomers is likely to mean a diminishing of—and possibly an outright end to—the kind of stereotyping that currently limits people over 65."

As America matures, senior citizens will constitute a larger voting block, labor force, and consumer group than before. Some politicians, employers, and advertisers consider this bloc a beneficial resource. They envision senior citizens contributing by exerting political pressure and increasing the nation's productivity. The elderly will also aid the economy by spending more on goods and services.

Others focus on the burdens an aging society presents. In *The New York Times*, Jonathan Peterson and Robert A. Rosenblatt state, "The growing elderly population will place new strains on the political system. Workers will face a rising tax burden to pay for medical care and retirement benefits."

Confronting the demands of an aging population that is eager to secure health care, political power, and the right to work will remain problematic. Faced with these demands, society has begun to adopt various, often conflicting views of the elderly. The viewpoints in this chapter examine some of these perceptions.

"To be poor and elderly is to be rendered utterly worthless by the standards of our society."

The Elderly Are Mistreated by Society

Pat Moore with Marty Jerome

Pat Moore founded Moore & Associates, an industrial design firm with offices in New York and New Jersey. Marty Jerome is the associate editor of *New Age Journal*, a monthly magazine. In the following viewpoint, Moore explains how her professional interest in design led her to dress up as an elderly woman. From this experience, the authors conclude that to be elderly is to be tormented and abused by a society that values youth above all else.

As you read, consider the following questions:

1. How did shopkeepers respond to Moore when she went into stores as an elderly woman?
2. How did other elderly people react to Moore when she dressed as an old woman, according to the authors?
3. What is the underlying reason abuse of the elderly occurs, in the authors' view?

Pat Moore with Marty Jerome, "Gray Like Me: A Young Woman's Experiment with Aging," *New Age Journal*, March/April 1988. Reprinted by permission of author.

As I watch a bag lady sitting silently and motionless on the park bench she frequents day after day, I am swept with a familiar, haunting pain. I know that she is only one of a growing number of impoverished elderly people living in our cities, alone and helpless, all but invisible. I say invisible because that's how it feels to be abjectly ignored not only by passers-by, but by a society obsessed with materialism and youth. I should know how it feels. I used to be an elderly woman.

Those few who knew of my double life were understandably concerned. Certainly, walking around New York City dressed as a woman of eighty-five years was peculiar behavior for my mere twenty-five years. But it was also dangerous. My experiment would provide me with moments of joy as well as the agony of being beaten unconscious and permanently injured.

Being elderly is something you can't truly understand until you've been there yourself. I had professional reasons for wanting to find out more about it. As an industrial designer, I am responsible for the creation of new products for everyday use. One of my first projects after college involved the design of a refrigerator. The design was one my grandmother would have found impossible to use because of her arthritis. I pointed out the design's limitations, arguing that we could accommodate consumers of all ability levels, if we tried.

Ignoring the Needs of the Elderly

The prevailing wisdom, however, held that my grandmother was not a "normal" consumer, so her needs weren't significant enough to take into consideration. Something was wrong with Grandma, not the design. This made no sense to me whatsoever. So I set out to learn more, first with classes in biomechanics at New York University and in gerontology at Columbia University, and then with my three-year adventure as an elder.

I wanted to design products that fully accommodated the needs of all members of society, but first I had to personally come to terms with those needs. As I walked down the street one day, concentrating on my feet, it occurred to me that the simple experience of walking, for example, would be completely different if I were older. With that, I realized just what my next step would involve.

With the help of my good friend Barbara Kelly, then a makeup designer for NBC Television, I was catapulted into the future. Barbara's work was masterful. From prefab jowls, crow's feet, bags for under my eyes, to the extra skin for my neck, the bindings on my legs—even the baby oil dabbed into my eyes to glaze them—the transformation was astonishing. I was so convincing, in fact, that I knew from my first time "in character" that I was onto something that would teach me far-reaching lessons about being elderly . . . and about myself.

One of the first things I learned is that money indeed talks. While the poor are often treated shabbily anyway, to be poor *and* elderly is to be rendered utterly worthless by the standards of our society. I was able to discover this by dressing up as an elder woman of various economic and social levels.

When I wasn't being ignored as a poor older woman, I was greeted with condescension, impatience, and hostility. Shopkeepers wanted me out of their stores. People on the street avoided me like I was vermin—as if poverty and old age were contagious. Clerks refused to help me, or even to answer my questions. The isolation was numbing, a kind of psychological torture. When I see elderly street people today, I realize that their despondency and peculiar behavior owe largely to the kind of treatment to which they're subjected.

Among the elderly themselves, however, I found a tacit sense of unity, an unspoken understanding that they have been collectively mistreated by society. The Gray Panthers Project Fund and other highly visible organizations exemplify only one part of that understanding and unity. Far more widespread are the unorganized networks of support among our elders. A small example of this touched my life one day in a way that made me under-

SOCIETY'S TARGETS

© Germano/Rothco

stand how extremely important these grass-root networks are.

Upon returning home one afternoon still in character, I opened the mail and found the papers that finalized my divorce. The emotional force of the documents struck me as hard as had the actual separation. I was unable to muster even enough energy to change out of the old Pat. So I left my empty apartment and wandered over to Washington Square Park. I sat on a bench looking like a weeping elderly woman, feeling like an isolated and discarded young woman.

"Is there anything I can do to help, dear?" came a voice from overhead. I looked up to see the warm eyes of an older woman beaming down at me. "Would I be intruding if I joined you?" she said. I moved my cane so that she could sit down and then explained how my marriage had ended after eight years.

"You loved him very much?" she asked, putting her hand on mine. "I never married. I was in love once, but he died in the war." She paused and sighed. "I never found anyone like him."

My anguish subsided, and we chatted until almost dusk.

I never saw the woman again, but the time she spent with me provided an emotional healing that was available nowhere else. Hers was the kind of concern that the young Pat needed, an exchange much more common between older people than between people with less life experience.

As the older Pat became a comfortable alter identity, I began to grapple with several internal conflicts. I was changing into character every other day during this period, moving in and out of elderly circles, getting to know and care about several individuals. The trouble was, I could only allow these relationships to develop to a limited point because I was representing someone who didn't actually exist. I felt cruel terminating friendships that I really wanted to let flourish. What I didn't realize at the time was that I was also cheating myself.

Meeting George

One day I was sitting in the park when an older man approached and asked if he could join me. I nodded my consent, and he sat down, pulling a piece of candy from a paper bag and offering it to me.

He introduced himself with a tip of his hat as George. We made small talk about the approaching autumn, and George told me that he used to take long drives with his wife during this time of year.

"We used to go upstate just to see the colors," he said. "She's gone now. She used to tell me, 'George, life's for the living! You promise me you won't waste it.' It's been three years and two months since she died." His voice tightened and wavered, and he took a quick swipe at his eyes with his handkerchief, hoping I wouldn't notice.

20

"I'm not married either, George," I said. "And I think we have something in common. It's a strange feeling to love someone, live with someone, then suddenly be alone. I wonder if I'll ever get accustomed to it."

We met at the same bench every Tuesday for several weeks, sometimes taking lunch, sometimes just passing time together. It began to occur to me that more than a friendship was developing, that in fact, we were dating. I was pleased with the idea, but I couldn't bring myself to reveal my real identity. He was courting the older Pat, after all, not the younger. I didn't want to jeopardize our friendship.

Shunning the Needy

There are elders who for one reason or another have "fallen between the cracks" in our social service and mental health programs. They may be alone, without living family, or at least without anyone who cares about them in particular. Their need for care and for caretakers is desperate. . . .

Those not directly affected by these troubled and needy elders prefer not to become involved. The presence of these social outcasts reflects our inability to provide adequate care, which, in turn, testifies to our society's lack of genuine social concern. We don't like the spotlight to be focused on our failures. The alternative is to turn away, to shun, to avoid, and to protect our unconcern by claiming a lack of knowledge.

Gerald A. Larue, *The Humanist*, July/August 1989.

One Tuesday George didn't arrive as planned. The following Tuesday I waited for him again and he failed to come. I was desperate with worry. He could have been ill. Maybe he needed my help. As I sat on the bench waiting and worrying, I began to understand the extent of our relationship. It was love in the truest sense. As the sun went down, I began to make my way out of the park, on the verge of tears, not knowing George's surname, unable to locate him. More than anything else, I was beginning to feel alone and forgotten. I never saw George again, though I continue to look.

Young people tend to focus on what they see as the disadvantages of being older, believing that above all else, to be old is to be ugly. This is astounding to me. I see a tremendous, unrecognized beauty in the process of aging. And yet, as a culture we remain frightened by this, frightened of dealing with our own evolution, with our future. And we project this fear onto our elders.

Unfortunately this fear and alienation can surface in far more horrifying ways than in merely subjecting older people to isolation. One day, while in character in New York, I emerged from a restaurant, startled to see most of the daylight gone. It made me uneasy. As an elder, I knew the danger of being alone on the street at night. I decided that the fastest way home was to cross through an unfamiliar neighborhood to get to Park Avenue where I could hail a cab.

A short walk for a healthy, limber individual can become a tedious trek for someone challenged with a body changed by time or circumstance. The bindings on my legs reduced my mobility and enhanced my sympathy. I walked slowly, deliberately, as so many of us will one day. And I moved in fear.

Suddenly, I felt a terrific blow from behind. Someone grabbed me by the neck, jerked me backwards, and threw me to the ground. A foot slammed into my stomach. The pain was so intense I thought I was going to black out. The boys grabbed my purse, but instead of running away, they danced around me, jeering, kicking me viciously from all sides. I remember thinking that I wouldn't live through this, that they had seriously injured me, and that if I did survive, I would never be able to have a baby. I passed out.

Had I been an elderly woman, I might not have survived that night. Today, as a woman of thirty-five, my body reflects the damage of the attack. I still have trouble moving all the fingers on one hand. But with the pain has come revelation. Nothing calls into question our very humanity, our core as beings, more than the abuse of those who can't defend themselves.

Abuse of the Elderly

Instead of being immobilized by my attack, I was empowered by it. It catapulted me into the fight against abuse of the elderly, what has become part of my life course. . . .

In city after city, the elderly I spoke with while I was in character confirmed some of my worst fears. Since 1979, I have listened to hundreds of stories of abuse, occurring not just in nursing homes, but at the hands of elders' spouses, and most often, by their children. . . .

Producing a generation of youngsters who value and appreciate their elders is the long-term solution to the problems the elderly face. But there are more immediate concerns. Senior citizens comprise the fastest growing segment of our society. Our corporate and business communities have been surprisingly slow to respond to their consumer needs. Only when the marketplace demands it will industry begin to relate to the lives of all people, regardless of age or ability.

"Far more than a majority of the elderly go through each day without frequent difficulties, serious problems, or worrisome fears."

The Elderly Are Not Mistreated by Society

Leslie Lenkowsky

In the following viewpoint, Leslie Lenkowsky argues that social programs such as Social Security have significantly improved the lives of the elderly. To further support his point, Lenkowsky cites polls which show that most elderly feel they have few serious problems or worries. Lenkowsky is president of the Institute for Educational Affairs, adjunct professor of public policy at Georgetown University and an adjunct scholar of the American Enterprise Institute for Public Policy Research, all of which are in Washington, D.C. He has also worked in government agencies and writes and lectures frequently on social policy, philanthropy, and education.

As you read, consider the following questions:

1. To what factors does Lenkowsky attribute the elderly's improved standard of living?
2. Why is the media's portrayal of the elderly inaccurate, according to the author?
3. Why does Lenkowsky believe that the few elderly who are poor are not in a desperate state?

Leslie Lenkowsky, "Why Growing Old is Getting Better," *Public Opinion*, May/June 1987. Reprinted with the permission of the American Enterprise Institute for Public Policy Research.

High on any list of Hollywood's all-time tear-jerkers would undoubtedly be a now-forgotten movie, *Make Way for Tomorrow.* The movie, starring Victor Moore and Beula Bondi, appeared in the mid-1930s. It told the story of an endearing elderly couple in the midst of the Great Depression, living together in their own home, seemingly in good health but facing the prospect of their declining years with no one to care for them. Their children, beset by their own concerns or living too far away, showed no eagerness to be helpful. In the end, after much family agonizing, the parents accept the inevitable. Not an eye could have possibly stayed dry as Moore finally placed his wife on a train to *her* nursing home, while he prepared to board a different one to *his.*

Just as this film was prompting a run on Kleenex, the Roosevelt administration was drafting legislation that aimed to make such family dramas a thing of the past. Though also concerned with the unemployed, the main purpose of the Social Security Act of 1935 was to ensure that the elderly would have enough to live on after retirement. Because so many were thought to have exhausted their savings (or lost them in a bank collapse), to have inadequate financial support from their children, and to dread the prospect of going to local welfare officials for relief, poverty in old age became a major concern. The 1935 law was designed to deal with the problem and, by most accounts, it has done so successfully.

According to the official Census Bureau statistics, fewer than one in seven people above the age of sixty-five were poor in 1985. If in-kind benefits, such as food stamps, Medicare, and Medicaid were taken into account, the elderly poverty rate might drop below 3 percent. To no small extent, the increasing value of social security benefits has had much to do with the steady decline in poverty among the elderly since the 1960s. Indeed, without the program, close to half the aged might be poor. As Senator Daniel P. Moynihan has observed, "Social security has removed much of the fear of growing old."

Old Myths

Nonetheless, the belief that the "golden years" are not really so golden dies hard, especially on television. After reviewing nearly 150 stories on the aged that were broadcast by the network nightly news shows between 1980 and 1985, the University of Rochester's Bruce Jacobs concluded, "The vast majority of segments in which individual old people are portrayed have as a central theme some form of deprivation or victimization." And even though many commentators have also noted the improved well-being of the elderly, a 1985 *Los Angeles Times* poll found that two-thirds of the public thought the percentage of old people living in poverty was increasing.

More recently the Villers Foundation [now Families USA Foundation], a Washington, D.C. charity that assists the aged, issued a report aimed at disproving the supposedly growing myth that the elderly are "living very well—at the expense of everyone else." To the contrary, argued the report, even after counting social security benefits, a vast portion of older Americans—42 percent—are poor or close to it and are "economically vulnerable." (That is, have annual incomes below $10,312 for an individual and $13,006 for a couple—twice the poverty line.) Moreover, many of the elderly incur extraordinarily high expenses for medical care, leaving them in greater need than the poverty figures alone suggest.

Healthier and More Active

Americans are living longer than ever before, and older Americans are healthier, more active, more vigorous, and more influential than any other older generation in history.

Ken Dychtwald with Joe Flower, *New Age Journal*, January/February 1989.

While social security and other programs have helped enormously, major gaps in the safety net remain. Generally, no more than a third of the elderly estimated to be eligible receive aid from means-tested programs like supplemental security income (SSI), Medicaid, and food stamps. Budgetary measures (such as the 1983 delay in cost-of-living adjustments for social security and increases in what Medicare recipients must pay out-of-pocket for hospital bills) have also hurt older people.

Far from having done too much, we still have far to go to defeat "the ancient economic foes of the elderly: poverty, economic vulnerability, fear, uncertainty." According to the Villers Foundation, "Too many Americans spend their last years living in shadow on the wrong side of Easy Street." To brighten their lives, however, we must first "rid the neighborhood of a few myths."

Few Worries

If that is really the case, the place to start may have to be with the elderly themselves. For, at the same time the Villers Foundation was issuing its gloomy assessment, a Louis Harris poll of the aged conducted for the Commonwealth Fund Commission on Elderly People Living Alone revealed a different picture. Only one in seven older people reported that not having enough money to live on was a "serious problem." Slightly more (17 percent) felt they had too many medical bills. Similar proportions were concerned about being in poor health or needing money in the future. Altogether, according to the Harris poll, far more than a majority of the elderly go through each day without frequent difficulties, serious problems, or worrisome fears.

But what about the minority who do encounter such troubles? Roughly half, it turns out, say they get the help they need. This is especially true for physical problems, such as going shopping or cooking meals; of those who require help, hardly anyone fails to get it. Approximately one-third reported that they received needed financial assistance; those who did not amounted to less than 10 percent of all the elderly. This is about half the number estimated to be eligible for SSI who for one reason or another are not claiming it.

To be sure, the Harris survey concluded that, based on reported income, 21 percent of the elderly were living below the poverty-line. Three-quarters of this group, however, said they did *not* regard themselves as having been poor before reaching age sixty-five; no effort was made to determine how many thought of themselves as poor when polled. Furthermore, more than half of the aged poor said they did not have even one serious problem or worry, and of those who did, many appeared able to obtain help.

A More Realistic Picture

The portrait of the elderly that emerges from this survey is certainly not one of a group living on "Easy Street." But it is not one of vast distress and "economic vulnerability" either. More than 90 percent say they are "satisfied" with their lives. Indeed, the most startling finding in the Harris poll is that the aged seem to be four times more likely to *give* financial assistance to family members and friends than to receive it. In stark contrast to the 1930s, when the elderly relied on the charity of their children, a large segment of today's elderly are likely to find their children or other relatives relying on them.

Not all older people are so fortunate. Both the Harris survey and the Villers Foundation report pay particular attention to the plight of the elderly who live by themselves. Typically widows in their eighties, this group is considerably more likely to be poor, infirm, and without close relatives. For them, growing old does indeed entail increasing hardships, often culminating in institutionalization and loss of independence.

Nonetheless, though the plight of these so-called "old-old" (age 85 and above) is tragic, it is important to put it in perspective. In the first place, the proportion of all elderly who are poor and living alone is small—roughly 8 percent, according to Harris. (The number above the age of eighty is smaller still.) Moreover, all are people who worked (or whose spouses worked) at a time when private pensions and deferred savings plans were less widely available. Hence, a smaller portion have income besides social security than is the case with the "young-old." Not least important, efficient ways of helping this group—means-tested programs like SSI and Medicaid—are already in place. Indeed, nearly 40 percent of the elderly, the Harris survey reports, would be willing to have their own social security benefits reduced in order to provide more assistance to the aged who live in poverty. What may stand in the way of such a solution is the reluctance of many of the "old-old"—who came of age during the Depression—to accept help from programs that are reminiscent of "relief."

The Perception and Reality of Aging

It is a well-established impression in the United States that older people suffer from inadequate income, ill health, loneliness, above-average rates of crime, and other social and economic problems. In fact, older Americans are no more prone to these troubles than is any other age group; and in a number of areas they are better off than average.

Henry J. Aaron, *The Brookings Review*, Summer 1986.

Ironically, the worry now expressed by foundations and policy makers about people who live independently into their eighties is a considerable tribute to the progress the elderly have made. No longer is assuring financial security their main problem; rather, coping with the inevitable consequences of a longer life span— social and medical as well as economic—is. This is a more difficult matter, and we may find that the very independence social security and other programs have permitted and encouraged hinders our efforts at a solution. But that is in the future. In the meantime, it will do no good pretending that a large proportion of the elderly still live in circumstances not far removed from the past, when reaching the age of sixty-five might have meant being carted off to a nursing home—if one was lucky.

"America's senior citizens are suddenly flexing their biceps in presidential politics."

Elderly Voters Influence American's Elections

Margot Hornblower

In the following viewpoint, written during the 1988 presidential campaign, Margot Hornblower describes how senior citizens have organized into effective special-interest political groups. In this way, Hornblower writes, the elderly are helping to shape the course of American politics and demanding that the federal government respond to their needs. Hornblower is a New York correspondent for *Time*, a national weekly newsmagazine.

As you read, consider the following questions:

1. What tactics does the American Association for Retired Persons use to influence election outcomes, according to Hornblower?
2. How does the author describe election candidate responses to elderly organizations?
3. What does Hornblower contend are crucial issues for the elderly?

Margot Hornblower, "Gray Power!" *Time*, January 4, 1988. Copyright 1988 Time Inc. Reprinted by permission.

An older woman strides confidently through the local head-quarters of the American Association of Retired Persons and looks straight at the television camera. "AARP's 27 million members believe that together, we can make a difference," she says. "We'll make sure you know what the candidates say—and what they don't say—about issues." Her tone is sweetly reasonable. But just to make sure those video-dazed viewers in Iowa and New Hampshire sit up and listen, she shakes her spectacles at them and adds, "If you think you've seen it all, you ain't seen nothin' yet."

Blunt and a tad belligerent, America's senior citizens are suddenly flexing their biceps in presidential politics. Flush from a Capitol Hill victory that protected Social Security increases from the budget ax, the Gray Lobby has turned its muscle to states where early contests will winnow the field of presidential candidates. Across the country, campaign operatives report that no other group has emerged in this election cycle with such unexpected force. "Any candidate who wants to win in 1988 is not going to mess with the old folks," says Thomas Kiley, an adviser to Michael Dukakis. . . .

Candidates, knowing that senior citizens flock to the polls with a vengeance, have responded with a gusher of saccharine rhetoric. "If we can get a man to the moon, we ought to be able to get dentures to people who built our society," went a sample line from Democrat Paul Simon at AARP's Iowa debate. The 1,000 gray-haired activists in attendance applauded noisily. On the way out, Wally Wakefield, a retired salesman from West Des Moines, couldn't help gloating. "They came because of us," he said. "We're powerful."

Founded in 1958 mainly to provide insurance for retirees, AARP is now the nation's largest special-interest group. "Join the Association that's bigger than most countries," boasted a recent magazine ad. This elderly behemoth, nearly twice the size of the AFL-CIO [American Federation of Labor and Congress of Industrial Organizations], continues to grow by about 8,000 new dues payers a day. One out of nine Americans belongs, paying a $5 annual fee. AARP offers drug and travel discounts, runs the nation's largest group-health-insurance program and a credit union. In addition, its savvy media operation includes *Modern Maturity*, the nation's third highest circulation magazine; a wire service that provides newspapers with "unbiased reporting" on elderly issues; and a weekly television series.

Given AARP's clout, the mere fact that it is distributing a voter's guide to its positions is enough to stun most Democratic and Republican hopefuls into obsequiousness. Filing through its beige-carpeted Washington headquarters, they submit to a grilling: Would they cut Social Security cost-of-living allowances? Would they support federal insurance for nursing-home care? Should

Medicare cover the cost of outpatient prescription drugs? So far, the candidates are telling AARP much of what it wants to hear. As Republican Jack Kemp put it, any politician who would tamper with Social Security is a "candidate for a frontal lobotomy."

Other organizations of elderly are also stepping up their political activity. In 1986 the National Council of Senior Citizens mounted "truth squads" of retirees that traveled the country publicizing incumbent Senators' votes on Social Security. In Iowa the National Committee to Preserve Social Security and Medicare has taken to guerrilla tactics, disrupting kaffeeklatsches and candidates' forums to push for higher benefits.

Such activism reflects a dramatic demographic trend. Since 1900 the total U.S. population has tripled while the number of elderly has risen eightfold. As today's baby boomers lurch into their 50s during the next decade, the numbers will explode further. The 1988 election "is a test case" for the elderly, said Mike McCurry, press secretary to Democratic Candidate Bruce Babbitt. "They will try to establish themselves as a political force, and if they do, they will alter the political landscape." Sixty-five-year-olds vote at nearly

"In a new turn, the government admitted making
arms sales to the Gray Panthers, with proceeds being
funneled into the Social Security system."

three times the rate of eligible voters under 24. In Iowa, whose population ranks among the oldest of any state, more than half the Democrats at the 1984 caucuses were over 50.

Gray Power is far from docile. One AARP television spot shows an oldster relentlessly interrupting a smooth-talking politician to pin him down on the issues. In fact, that's just what Michael Molnar, a retired security guard, whose wife requires $2,400 a month in nursing-home care for Alzheimer's disease, did to Democrat Albert Gore. As Gore wound up a speech at a Salem, N.H., nursing home, Molnar rose to ask: Did the Senator agree that our health-care system was a disgrace? And what was Gore's position on Senate Bill 1127? Did he support the prescription-drug plank? What about the long-term-nursing-care legislation? Gore responded that he favored the prescription-drug proposal but believed long-term nursing care was too expensive.

A testier encounter took place in Ottumwa, Iowa, between Dukakis and retired nurse Pauline Snelling, 65. Despite her red blazer plastered with Dukakis stickers, Snelling stalked out of a town meeting after the candidate brushed aside a question on "notch babies," the group of seniors born between 1917 and 1921 who got lower cost-of-living increases after Congress readjusted Social Security benefits in 1977. "It's not what he says about the country," she snorted. "What matters is how he answers these questions."

While campaign politicking may be a new frontier for seniors, their clout has long been felt in Washington. When congressional and Administration budget negotiators sought to cut the deficit in the wake of the [1987] Wall Street crash, they briefly considered a proposal to scale down Social Security cost-of-living increases. Congressman Claude Pepper, 87, held a press conference to announce that he would force a separate House vote on the issue. The Gray Lobby went to work. The result? Although programs for the elderly account for one-third of the budget, negotiators dropped the proposal in a fright. "These are people who have plenty of time on their hands, who are well organized, who vote regularly, and they are a massive political force," lamented Budget Director James Miller.

In the past AARP has exercised restraint; in 1985 it even endorsed the Senate Republican proposal of a one-time cost-of-living freeze on Social Security. But with the hiring of tough-talking lobbyist Jack Carlson as executive director, the group began to harden its stance, partly to prevent other organizations of the elderly from stealing the thunder. Next on AARP's agenda: a multibillion-dollar proposal for federal insurance to cover long-term at-home or nursing-home care. While other lobbies are often content with dumping a blizzard of preprinted postcards on Capitol Hill, AARP members tend to write their own letters. "AARP is the equivalent of an 800-lb. gorilla," says Congressman Hal Daub, a Republican on the Social Security subcommittee.

Although Paul Simon's recent surge in Iowa was interpreted as a boost from a constituency that still remembers Harry Truman, the retirees' vote seems up for grabs. So far the only candidates who have dared stray from the party line are those so far behind in the polls that they have little to lose. Bruce Babbitt talks of raising taxes on Social Security benefits of the affluent elderly. Pat Robertson and Pete du Pont warn that Social Security is threatened with bankruptcy and advocate shifting some of the burden to private plans. "When the baby-boom generation retires, we're going to have to double taxes on our kids or cut benefits in half," says du Pont.

But the front-running candidates pay fealty to the sanctity of Social Security and ardently embrace much of what the Gray Lobby advocates. Does this mean that AARP and the other groups will not unite behind a single candidate and that their impact may be somewhat diffused? Probably. But that in itself is a victory. It shows that their energetic new force has already helped shape the 1988 political agenda, and no doubt will continue to do so.

"The aged do not wield power as a single-issue voting constituency."

The Influence of Elderly Voters Is Exaggerated

Robert H. Binstock

Robert H. Binstock is the Henry R. Luce Professor of Aging, Health, and Society at the School of Medicine at Case Western Reserve University in Cleveland, Ohio. He was formerly president of the Gerontological Society of America. In the following viewpoint, Binstock argues that the elderly do not vote as a special interest group and have only minimal political power. The elderly cannot affect election outcomes or get legislation passed, according to Binstock.

As you read, consider the following questions:

1. What evidence does Binstock give that the elderly do not constitute a single-issue voting bloc?
2. How does the author account for the passage of old-age legislation?
3. What kinds of power do old-age interest groups have on the political process, according to Binstock?

Robert H. Binstock, "Aging, Politics and Public Policy." This article appeared in the December 1988 issue and is reprinted with permission of *The World & I*, a publication of The Washington Times Corporation. Copyright © 1988.

American public policy toward aging is approaching an important crossroads. Will public policies continue—as they have for several decades—to treat "the elderly" as a stereotyped group? If so, government expenditures on programs for the aging will grow at an enormous rate, but without alleviating the problems of those within the older population who are most seriously disadvantaged; at the same time, older persons may well be blamed for a host of problems in American society. Or will stereotypes weaken and public policies begin to focus on older Americans in all their diversity, providing effective help to those aging persons who need it most? . . .

The Aged as a Constituency

Will the elderly, per se, have sufficient political influence to control or veto proposed changes that appear detrimental to them? A brief examination of the sources and applications of the power available to the elderly suggests not.

Persons 65 and older do constitute a large bloc of participating voters. They represent 16.7 to 21 percent of those who actually voted in national elections during the 1980s. And this percentage is likely to increase in the next four decades because of projected increases in the proportion of older persons.

But older persons do not vote in a monolithic bloc, any more than middle-aged persons or younger persons do. Consequently, the aged do not wield power as a single-issue voting constituency.

Election exit polls have shown repeatedly that the votes of older persons distribute among candidates in about the same proportions as the votes of other age groupings of citizens. Although men and women can be seen to have distributed their votes in patterns, persons in the differing age categories of 30-44, 45-59, and 60 and older who cast their ballots in these elections did not. Examination of properly sampled exit polls from other national elections show the same result.

These data should not be surprising since there is no sound reason to expect that a cohort of persons would suddenly become homogenized in its political behavior when it reaches the "old age" category. Diversity among older persons may be at least as great with respect to political attitudes and behavior as it is in relation to economic, social, and other characteristics.

The very assumption that mass groupings of the American citizenry vote primarily on the basis of self-interested responses to single issues is, in itself, problematic. Candidates, not issues, run for office. In the context of choosing between candidates, a voter's response to any one issue is part of an overall response to a variety of issues in a campaign and to many other stimuli that may have little to do either with specific issues or with the presumed "self interest" that might be implied by a single issue.

34

Moreover, within a heterogeneous group such as older persons, self-interested responses to any single issue are likely to vary substantially. The best available studies show that even in the context of a state or local referendum that presents a specific issue for balloting—such as propositions to cap local property taxes or to finance public schools—old age is not a statistically significant variable associated with the distribution of votes.

Nationwide Vote Distribution, by Age Groups, in Recent Elections for the U.S. House of Representatives

	1982		1984		1986	
	Democrat	Republican	Democrat	Republican	Democrat	Republican
Percent of						
All Voters	57	43	51	49	52	48
Percent of Men						
18-29 years old	60	40	47	53	48	52
30-44 years old	52	48	52	48	52	48
44-59 years old	54	46	47	53	50	50
60 years & older	56	44	46	54	51	49
Percent of Women						
18-29 years old	58	42	56	44	54	46
30-44 years old	57	43	56	44	52	48
44-59 years old	58	42	52	48	58	42
60 years & older	60	40	51	49	53	47
Percent of Adults						
18-29 years old	59	41	51	49	51	49
30-44 years old	54	46	54	46	52	48
44-59 years old	56	44	50	50	54	46
60 years & older	58	42	48	52	52	48

Source: 1982, 1984, and 1986 nationwide exit polls conducted by *The New York Times/CBS News Poll*, published in *The New York Times*, Nov. 6, 1986, p. 15Y.

But don't politicians behave as if older persons vote as a bloc in response to issues? Aren't they terrorized by so-called senior power?

It is certainly evident that no politician goes out of his way to offend the aged. On the other hand, there have been numerous cases in recent years when Congress has enacted legislation that has adversely affected the presumed interests of the aged. At the outset of the 1980s, for example, Congress legislated five provisions narrowing benefits and eligibility under Social Security, which had an adverse effect on Old Age Insurance benefits. More recently, the Tax Reform Act of 1986 eliminated the extra personal exemption from federal income taxes that had been universally available to persons 65 and older.

Only limited power is available to the "Gray Lobby"—the aging-based mass-membership interest groups, such as the American Association of Retired Persons (AARP) and the National Council of Senior Citizens (NCSC)—and to dozens of other aging-based professional and business organizations "representing" older persons. As implied by the preceding discussion of electoral behavior, such organizations have not been able to cohere or even to marginally shift the votes of older persons. While AARP claims more than 28 million members, for example, it does not control or demonstrably influence the votes of these members. In the 1980 presidential campaign, the leaders of a number of major aging-based organizations vigorously endorsed President Carter in his bid for reelection. Nevertheless, a majority of older persons voted for his opponent, Ronald Reagan, and did so in the same proportion as voters in younger age groupings. . . .

Organized demands of older persons have had little to do with the enactment and amendment of the major old-age policies such as Social Security and Medicare. Rather, such actions have been largely attributable to the initiatives of public officials in the White House, Congress, and the bureaucracy, all of which have focused on their own agendas for social and economic policy. The impact of old-age-based interest groups has been largely confined to relatively minor policies, enacted from the mid-1960s to the mid-1970s, that have distributed benefits to professionals and practitioners in the field of aging rather than directly to older persons themselves.

Minimal Power

Some forms of power, however, are available to old-age interest groups. In the classic pattern of American interest-group politics, public officials find it both useful and incumbent upon them to invite such organizations to participate in policy activities. In this way, public officials are provided with a ready means of having been "in touch" with millions of constituents, thereby legitimizing subsequent policy actions and inactions. A brief meeting with the leaders of these organizations can enable an official to claim that he has duly obtained the represented views of a mass constituency.

Consequently, the legitimacy that old-age organizations have for participating in interest group politics gives them several forms of power. First, they have easy informal access to public officials, including members of Congress and their staffs, career bureaucrats, appointed officials, and, occasionally, the White House. They can put forth their own proposals—regarding Medicare, nursing home regulations, Social Security, and a variety of other matters—and work to block the proposals of others. To be sure, their audiences or targets may be unresponsive in subsequent policy decisions, but access provides some measure of opportunity.

Second, their legitimacy enables them to obtain public platforms in the national media, Congressional hearings, and in national conferences and commissions dealing with old age, health, and a variety of subjects relevant to policies affecting the elderly. From these platforms, the old-age organizations can exercise power by initiating and framing issues for public debate and by responding to issues raised by others.

Division Within AARP

AARP entered big-time politics late and hesitantly, recognizing that partisanship can rip its loosely knit fabric apart. A survey in 1984 revealed that 40% of the members are Democrats, 40% Republicans, and the rest independents. By expressing a presidential preference AARP would presumably make half its members unhappy. Playing it safe, AARP declines to finance or endorse any candidate.

Lee Smith, *Fortune*, February 29, 1988.

A third form of power available to these groups might be called "the electoral bluff." Although these organizations have not demonstrated a capacity to swing a decisive bloc of older voters, no politician wants to offend "the aged" or any other latent mass constituency if he can avoid doing so. In fact, the image of senior power is frequently invoked by politicians when—for one reason or another—they desire an excuse for doing nothing or for not differentiating themselves from their colleagues and electoral opponents.

Limited Impact

These forms of power, although minor when compared with the power available to organizations that are based upon major economic interests, appear to have some impact, however limited. Historically, as indicated earlier, the age-based organizations have not played an influential role in shaping Medicare, Social Security, and other major programs. The impact of these organizations has been confined largely to the creation and maintenance of relatively minor policies that have distributed benefits primarily to researchers, educators, clinicians, and other practitioners in the field of aging rather than directly to older persons themselves.

"The world of advertising is swiftly opening up to a more positive image of aging."

Advertisers Promote a Positive View of the Elderly

Ken Dychtwald and Joe Flower

In the following viewpoint, taken from the book *Age Wave*, Ken Dychtwald and Joe Flower argue that advertisers are rejecting negative stereotypes of the elderly in favor of new positive images that will attract elderly consumers. They argue that these new role models depicted in advertisements reflect more accurately how the elderly perceive themselves. Dychtwald is a gerontologist from Emeryville, California, and Flower is a free-lance writer based in Sausalito, California.

As you read, consider the following questions:

1. What examples do the authors give of positive images of the elderly in commercials?
2. What roles do older people play in the ads that Dychtwald and Flower cite?
3. How do companies predict the elderly market will respond to these ads, according to the authors?

Reprinted by arrangement with the author, Dr. Ken Dychtwald, from *Age Wave*, Jeremy P. Tarcher, 1989.

Older people are very sensitive to being portrayed negatively. When Wendy's fast-food chain featured Clara Peller in its "Where's the beef?" ad campaign, many older people were insulted by the commercial. "We don't look or act like that!" they angrily responded. They felt that Peller's performance fostered images of older people as silly, cranky, and funny looking.

With increasing concern about health and personal well-being, older consumers want products and services that will make them feel and look better physically, mentally, and socially. According to industry observer Len Albin,

> When a TV commercial shows older people acting like dopes (having a nervous breakdown because of loose-fitting dentures) or a little fuzzy in the head (as in the old Country Time Lemonade ad, which was subsequently changed), it doesn't move older viewers to try the product. In fact, any sort of advertising which segregates older people as "different" is insulting.

The world of advertising is swiftly opening up to a more positive image of aging. We can see this trend reflected in the increasing use of older Americans in commercials as authority figures, as lovable grandparents, and simply as people who have their own full, rich lives. According to Clay Edmonds, marketing director at Ogilvy & Mather Partners, "Rather than youth being the ideal in advertisements, as it used to be, health, vigor, alertness, and doing the most with what you have are now the ideals."

Promoting Age

A good example is a Clairol commercial featuring middle-aged "Dynasty" beauty Linda Evans. The opening line? "Let's face it—40 isn't fatal." And an advertisement promoting *Lear's* magazine reads "If You're under 40, Lie about Your Age!"

More and more commercials now show attractive and vital people of all ages. A middle-aged man in a bran commercial does aerobics while his wife cheers him on. A mature beauty in an Oil of Olay commercial says, "I'm about to wash a whole day's worth of aging away." A distinguished gentleman with thinning silver hair sells Riunite wine. An over-50 Sophia Loren sells perfume named after her, as well as eyeglass frames. A glamorous mature model describes Cover Girl's "Replenish" for "changing" skins, and then asks, "Who says you ever have to stop being a cover girl?"

Even Pepsi, which built its reputation on the youthful baby-boom generation, is growing up. The initial image of the Pepsi Generation—with the product touted as being "for those who think young"—reflected Madison Avenue's infatuation with youth. Although all of the original Pepsi ads featured lively, energetic, and youthful actors, more recently Pepsi has begun to reach out to the older consumer. Now, the "Pepsi Spirit" campaign presents consumers who span at least three generations, enjoying Pepsi side by side. According to Alan Pottasch, senior vice-president for creative services for Pepsico, Inc., in the 1960s "Everyone wanted to 'think young.' . . . More recently, we've tried to take the Pepsi Generation from meaning the group from 15 to 25 and expand it to mean the group from 15 to 75, provided their attitude toward life is a vital one."

Cutty Sark based a successful advertising campaign on three people: a man and a woman who looked about 40, and an elegant, well-dressed, silver-haired man about 70, appearing together as symbols of sophistication, good taste, and affluence. According to Warren Berger of the Food and Beverage Marketing Association: "The Cutty campaign wasn't specifically directed at older consumers, though they are important Scotch buyers. Instead, the older gent was used both as a model for success for younger buyers, and one who would also play well with older drinkers." According to Don Klein, president of the Howard-Marlboro agency, which created the ad, "The objective was not to show an older person, but to communicate the feeling of achievement. . . . The reviews from the trade were positive—and, apparently, so was the response from consumers. Cutty was the only brand that grew in share last year."

Catering to the Elderly

The activity and prosperity of America's retirees have not gone unnoticed on Madison Avenue. There was a time when advertisers behaved as though no one past middle age ever bought anything more durable than panty hose. No more. Few marketing experts can ignore the fact that Americans over 50 earn more than half the discretionary income in the country. . . . Major firms are forming special groups to study the senior market, and at least one company that offers ageless ads has opened. "My sense is we're on the leading edge right now," says Jerry Gerber of LifeSpan in Manhattan, "way out there, totally new, totally different."

Nancy R. Gibbs, *Time*, February 22, 1988.

When AT&T, MCI, and GTE Sprint went head-to-head in competition over the long-distance telephone market in 1985, many consumers were confused about which service was better. To calm their anxiety, the long-distance companies all decided to use older, more mature spokespersons. AT&T hired 63-year-old Cliff Robertson as their primary spokesman. MCI used 75-year-old Burt Lancaster and 51-year-old Joan Rivers for its ads, while GTE Sprint went for a sophisticated, seductive lady with obvious lines of experience in her forehead.

A successful series of California commercials for the Pacific Bell telephone company featured a positive look at two older men calling each other long-distance to reminisce about the course of their 60-year friendship. According to Robert Black, the creative director of Foote, Cone and Belding, the ad firm that created the commercials, "I enjoy older people, and I think they're a natural for this kind of campaign. You have 60 years of life to portray; they give you a natural story-telling device."

Popular McDonald's Ads

Two of the most clever and popular television ads oriented toward the 50+ market were created for the McDonald's Corporation. One, entitled "The New Kid," depicts an older man experiencing his first day at work at a McDonald's restaurant. In his new job, he has a grand time pleasing the customers while showing the younger workers a thing or two about his seasoned skill and stamina—to their great pleasure. Perhaps it was the positive feelings that this ad engendered that caused it to be named one of the five favorite commercials of the year in 1987.

The second was entitled "Golden Time" and was created by the Leo Burnett Advertising Agency. According to Gene Mandarino, senior vice-president/creative director, "Everything on the tube is so 'up' and youthful. Everybody's jiving around in their Levi's. So when I was looking for an idea for McDonald's, I thought, 'Let's throw a change-up at them.' One-third of McDonald's customers are older people, but nobody talks about them."

The idea for "Golden Time" did not come from McDonald's, or from focus groups, surveys, or other market-sampling techniques. It sprang from Mandarino's own experience. "When I was living in the city, I used to see dozens of older people on the verandah of the McDonald's nearby," he says. "The people were so happy, the place was clean and comfortable, they could afford it. And I found myself wishing my dad had had a place like that in his neighborhood when he was alive. My father had lost my mother and was alone. He spent his last 15 years wandering through life, trying to find some companionship, feeling very clumsy about it."

Mandarino feels that "Golden Time" was a "sweet classic." He explains: "An older man walks into a McDonald's, past an older woman sitting alone in the corner. It's filmed close, intimate. There's music; he's seen her there before, he'd like to meet her, but he doesn't know what he'll say. He's as nervous as an adolescent. She's noticed him, too, the song tells us: 'I'm too old to be smitten; besides, it's not fittin'.' But this time he does work up the courage. He asks her if the space is taken, and as the curtain comes down, they are beginning a relationship.

"It was a commercial that people noticed, because it treated older people not as buffoons, but as real people."

"Most advertisers see seniors as frugal, stubborn and closed-minded."

Advertisers Promote a Negative View of the Elderly

Eva Pomice

In the following viewpoint, Eva Pomice describes how advertisers persist in producing negative images of the elderly that senior citizens find offensive. Concerned with capturing a youthful market, she writes, these advertisers are neglecting an important community of elderly consumers. Pomice works as an associate editor for *U.S. News & World Report.*

As you read, consider the following questions:

1. How do older people respond to negative advertising images, according to Pomice?
2. In the author's view, why do advertisers use negative images of the elderly?
3. What incentives does Pomice describe that could encourage advertisers to produce more positive images of the elderly?

Eva Pomice, "Madison Avenue's Blind Spot." Copyright, October 3, 1989, U.S. News & World Report.

Remember Clara Peller? The crusty grandmother's outraged cry of "Where's the beef?" raised Wendy's sales in the famous 1984 promotion. But the ad itself also raised hackles among Peller's contemporaries. The elderly figure recklessly speeding from one burger drive-in to the next insulted senior citizens by portraying them as crotchety and ridiculous and as bad drivers.

The Peller ads weren't alone. In fact, in a survey by advertising agency Ogilvy & Mather, 40 percent of the over-65-year-old respondents agreed that Madison Avenue usually presents older people as unattractive and incompetent. "Advertising shows young people at their best and most beautiful," says Treesa Drury, advertising-standards director for *Modern Maturity* magazine. "But it shows older people at their worst."

Neglecting the Elderly

Catering to a society fixated on youth, Madison Avenue has long neglected older Americans. Most advertisers see seniors as frugal, stubborn and closed-minded. Advertisers have compounded the problem, many industry critics charge, by showing older people as sickly and silly, rather than portraying them in the positive light in which many seniors see themselves.

None of these negative images seem warranted. Seniors as a group have money and aren't afraid to spend it. "People 50 and older have survived orthodontia and house payments and are more than willing to reward themselves," says Richard Balkite, Donnelley Marketing's director of senior marketing. People over 50 earn 42 percent of all total after-tax income and control half the nation's discretionary-spending power. A Donnelley study shows that mature consumers are much more interested in trying new brands and products than marketers had previously assumed.

Old Images

Despite such golden buying power, many ads still invoke stale and offensive stereotypes of seniors. A Subaru spot features its own feckless grandmother sneaking away from her rocker to take a spin around the block in Dad's new rocket. An ad for Denny's shows two frumpy old sisters; one of them is too hard of hearing to get the name of the restaurant right. Other commercials play too much on the fears and embarrassments of growing older. In an insurance ad, Danny Thomas pats the hand of an infirm senior citizen in a hospital bed and warns viewers not to wait "until it's too late." Says Leonard Hansen, chairman of Senior World Publications, "Few marketers communicate to older adults as successful humans who have accomplished a great deal in their lives."

One explanation for such failings may be the relative youth of Madison Avenue's marketers and copywriters. Critics claim that they have failed to recognize the gap between a person's chronological age and the psychological age, typically 15 years less.

"People do not grow old; their bodies betray them," says Jay Jasper, creative director at Ogilvy & Mather. "If you want to sell something to a man over 50, you don't put him in a cardigan, because cardigans are what grandpas wear." Direct references to age also doom many product pitches. A now legendary blunder was Johnson & Johnson's 1983 introduction of Affinity, a shampoo for "older" hair. Analyst James Gollub of SRI International recommends against "age typing" phrases such as golden oldies and golden years.

Distorted Images

Of the few elders who do appear on TV in one or another capacity, noted Marsel Heisel [who teaches gerontology at Rutgers University School of Social Work in New Jersey], almost all are male: only one in ten characters judged to be 65 or older is a woman. Thus, she said, if we assume that what has meaning and status for society finds its way onto television screens, the message conveyed seems to be that the elderly are not very important, and that among that population group, only men have significance. In referring to research of other gerontologists, Heisel also observed that when older persons do appear on screen, they tend to be "more comical, stubborn, eccentric, and foolish than other characters." She also cited a 1977 Annenberg School of Communication survey of more than 9,000 television characters, which determined that only 3.7 of them were elderly; moreover, compared to other groups, these individuals were portrayed as ineffective, unattractive and unhappy. . . .

What with all the media interest the elderly demonstrate, it is doubly cruel that the images they see of themselves therein are so frequently distorted. This fact itself can become a self-fulfilling prophecy, for people often act in the ways they are expected to. Their own self-images tend to conform to the images they see portrayed, thus setting up a vicious circle that seems well-nigh impenetrable.

Linda-Marie Delloff, *The Christian Century*, January 7-14, 1987.

Advertisers fear that an old-age image is the *coup de grâce* for mass-market products. Marketers could avoid that pitfall by using older actors in family and social settings, suggests David Ward, planning director at Ogilvy & Mather. Cereal makers like General Mills and Quaker Oats have included people over 50 in a crop of recent ads. Ralph Lauren pictures elegant older American women as part of a family dynasty. Marketers have been most successful with seniors, however, when they have touted the financial and personal freedom that comes with growing older, and stressed romance and glamour. McDonald's, for example, made a hit with the over-65 set with a romantic spot showing an old man bold enough to sit next to a comely older woman. An American Airlines print ad for its Senior Savers Club shows an attractive couple with windblown hair in a powerboat.

Overcoming Preconceptions

To some analysts, such ads presage real recognition by Madison Avenue of America's fastest-growing age group. But skeptics doubt whether an industry hooked so long on the elixir of youth can overcome its preconceptions, even to capture so golden a market.

"Caregivers suffer from depression, anxiety, frustration, helplessness, sleeplessness, and sheer emotional exhaustion."

The Elderly Are a Burden to Their Children

Grace W. Weinstein

In the following viewpoint, Grace W. Weinstein describes the disruptions and problems that families encounter when forced to care for an elderly parent. In addition, she notes that community services are usually incapable of providing much help. Weinstein is a contributing editor for the monthly *Ms.* magazine.

As you read, consider the following questions:

1. How are women particularly affected by the responsibility of caring for elderly parents, according to Weinstein?
2. What kinds of problems does the author believe caregivers face?
3. Why are community services unable to alleviate the burden of family care, in Weinstein's opinion?

The statistics are staggering:
- One in eight Americans is over age 65. By the year 2030, one in five will be over 65.
- The fastest growing segment of the elderly population consists of men and women (mostly women) over age 85. Fully half of this group requires assistance with daily living due to chronic illness or disability.
- At least 80 percent of the people needing long-term care receive it from family and friends. Social services targeted to this need are few and far between, and help in paying for those services is virtually nonexistent.
- The average woman will spend 17 years caring for children and 18 years caring for aged parents. In between, or simultaneously, she may spend years caring for an ill or disabled spouse.

The Harsh Reality

Sheila Gallagher (not her real name) began to learn the harsh reality behind these statistics when she was awakened one Sunday morning at six by a frantic telephone call from her 77-year-old mother. "She said she'd been waiting for me for dinner for hours, but that was only the beginning," says Gallagher. "Later that day she called into another room to ask my father, who'd been dead for eleven years, whether he was planning to mow the lawn."

You've heard about the "mommy track." Now brace yourself for the "daughter track," identified in a study by *Fortune* magazine and John Hancock Financial Services as a path populated by women who devote so much time to care of the elderly, usually a parent, that their careers are threatened. Men care for parents too. But study after study shows that men more often help with the checkbook or keep in touch by telephone. Women provide personal hands-on care: they cook, do housework, administer medicine, shepherd parents to the doctor. They also bathe them, dress them, change them, and feed them. Not infrequently, women provide such care for more than one aging relative—parents, in-laws (sometimes even after divorcing their son), aunts, and, eventually, their own husbands.

"The empty nest is nothing more than a myth," says Lou Glasse, president of the Older Women's League (OWL), referring to the assumption that women who have finished raising children can finally put their own needs first. "If women's 'nests' empty at all, they fill again very quickly with elderly parents or other relatives who need care and support."

Right now, according to a study sponsored by the American Association of Retired Persons and the Travelers Companies Foundation, up to 7 million people, 75 percent of them women, are providing care for an average of 12 hours a week and have been doing so for at least two years. More than half of these caregivers hold paying jobs, but other studies show that many caregivers, burdened with overwhelming responsibility, give up their jobs or cut back on working hours to the point where they lose out on their own health and retirement benefits. Such "volunteer" caregiving, says Glasse, is "a prime cause of the poverty that so many women endure in old age."

The Aging of the Baby Boomers

As the saying goes, though, we ain't seen nothin' yet. "Child care is still overshadowing elder care as an issue, and probably will for the next five to seven years," says Dana Friedman of the Families and Work Institute. Like a snake swallowing a mouse, the focus will begin to shift as the parents of the baby boom generation move into their seventies. The oldest baby boomer is now 43, her mother 65. The real crunch, the point at which the need for support services will become obvious to the most myopic politican, will come when the baby boom generation itself is elderly.

Feeling Guilty

What you hear caregiving women say over and over again—and it gives me goose bumps—is: "My mother took care of me when I was little, and now it's my turn." (Another thing you hear is that "we take care of the old in *our* ethnic group—it's one of *our* values." The funny thing is that you hear that from virtually every ethnic group.) Women are quick to assume that if they're under pressure, it's their own fault, for not managing things better. Even in extreme cases—where the aged parent is incontinent, where the parent has Alzheimer's disease and sets fires and shoplifts and makes scenes in public because she doesn't recognize the child and thinks she's being kidnapped—even there, the caregivers feel guilty.

I honestly don't know why we feel that way, but I do know it's not realistic. Old people are *not* babies. You'll never be able to feel toward your mother as you do toward your child, because it's a different relationship. A baby that wets its pants is going to grow up. With an old person you know it's all downhill.

Elaine Brody, *Ms.*, January 1986.

The caregiver today, however, has no time to take in the big picture. When Sheila Gallagher's mother began to show signs of dementia—a mental condition compounded, as it often is, by physical problems—she couldn't be left alone. "Mom needed someone to stay with her at night after she became very agitated and wandered two miles away," says Gallagher. "Eventually she needed someone all day." Gallagher tried to function at work while arranging care for her mother. That meant endless hours on the telephone with doctors, day care facilities, and home health agencies—calls that for an employed woman are made at lunchtime. "I've been so stressed out," she said one April day. "I haven't had a day off since November or gone out for lunch more than three times in the last year. It's like another full-time job. It's put a complete stop to my life."

Like many caregivers, Gallagher is doing everything possible to keep her mother at home instead of in a nursing home. Only 5 percent of those over 65 are in nursing homes at any one time because both the elderly and most of their relatives prefer home to institutional care. But marshaling support for home care takes its toll.

Emotional Exhaustion

Caregivers describe depleted wallets. They also report aching backs and pulled muscles from lifting. Most of all, whether providing hands-on care themselves or supervising paid help, they display emotional fatigue. With less time to spend with their own families, interruptions on the job, postponed vacations, and altered retirement plans, it's little wonder that caregivers suffer from depression, anxiety, frustration, helplessness, sleeplessness, and sheer emotional exhaustion.

They also feel guilt about not doing "enough," and guilt is a great inhibitor. It keeps you from demanding help and makes you personalize the problem. As Stephen McConnell, national coordinator of the Long Term Care Campaign, puts it, "In the past, long-term care was an issue families struggled with quietly in their own homes, out of a sense of guilt and responsibility. They haven't viewed it as something to talk to legislators about." But the need for long-term care services is coming out of the closet and emerging as a hot political issue. It's time to demand help.

Navigating the Maze

The key elements of elder care are nursing homes, home health care, adult day care, and respite services. "Unfortunately," as OWL's Lou Glasse sums up the situation, "very little outside help is available. That which does exist is expensive, of poor quality, or both." Existing services are so inadequate, at least in part, because people can't pay for them; most observers agree that when financing mechanisms are in place, services will follow.

The average annual cost of a nursing home is now $25,000 a year; some cost upward of $50,000 a year. At the same time, the median family income of the elderly is about $20,000 a year, while older women living alone have a median income of about $7,000. Beds are often in short supply, with national occupancy rates exceeding 90 percent. As for quality, although legislation passed by Congress in 1987 set standards for care for nursing homes receiving payment under either Medicare or Medicaid, implementation is lagging. Many provisions won't take effect until October 1990.

Confronting poor care is very difficult, because an elderly resident is vulnerable. "I complained about a nurse, but not as loudly as I might have," says one daughter, "because they have ways to get even. Dinner might be late, or cold, or she might handle my mother a bit more roughly than necessary."

A Woman's Responsibility

Families, especially adult daughters and daughters-in-law, provide most of the personal care and help with household tasks, transportation, and shopping for the elderly. Women particularly may have to leave the work force or work part-time to care for frail parents at just the time when they themselves are working to ensure the receipt of retirement benefits. As a result of delayed childbearing, many have responsibility for college-age children and frail parents, all while trying to hold a job or adjust to their own retirement, widowhood, and reduced incomes.

Cynthia M. Taeuber, *The World & I*, December 1988.

Although 42 states fund limited home care services, OWL reports that the programs serve only about 100,000 Americans while fully one million seriously disabled elderly living at home receive no assistance at all. Many caregivers are forced to place elderly relatives in nursing homes because there is so little support for at-home care.

At-Home Care

Even when at-home care is available and affordable, frequent turnover among poorly paid aides often means inadequate care. Home care workers earn so little and receive so few benefits that OWL has adopted their cause. The quality of care is affected as well by the lack of training and, given the isolated work sites, inadequate supervision that aides receive. Here, too, implementation of federal quality-of-care standards is slow. Neither home health aide training provisions nor toll-free home care hotlines are yet in place.

There are long waiting lists for adult day care programs, which can cost up to $50 a day or even more. Only 1,400 such centers exist nationwide, serving 66,000 persons. Many more of the elderly could benefit from the stimulation and socialization found in good day care; many more of their caregivers could benefit from time off.

Time off, in fact, is essential. Respite programs can make it possible for a full-time caregiver to get a haircut, visit the dentist, attend a wedding, take a vacation, retain her sanity. Programs specifically designed as respite for caregivers—as opposed to adult day care, which is designed primarily to benefit the elderly person—can run from an afternoon's at-home visit by a home health aide to a week-long stay in a nursing home. Yet Elaine M. Brody of the Philadelphia Geriatric Center, a *Ms.* Woman of the Year in 1985 known for her research on caregiving and "women in the middle," notes that instead of regular funding for respite programs, there are only "episodic and discontinuous efforts" to provide this sorely needed help.

One of the biggest problems family caregivers face is finding out where to find help. A hospital discharge planner can provide referrals if help is needed immediately after hospitalization. But elderly people often deteriorate without being hospitalized. The endless hours that the Sheila Gallaghers of this world spend on the telephone seeking help can be cut short by what social workers call a single "point of entry" into the system, a person or agency to determine just what services are needed and provide information on where to find them.

Private Geriatric Care Managers

The need is spurring the growth of a new profession: private geriatric care managers who assess need, coordinate services, and monitor care. Private care managers, often coming from social work or nursing backgrounds, are particularly helpful when long-distance caregiving is necessary—a service that Rona Bartelstone, a Miami-based care manager, says is typical of her practice. "But even when the family is nearby," says Bartelstone, president of the National Association of Private Geriatric Care Managers, "it might need help in knowing the options and establishing the best care plan."

Andi Klein (not her real name), herself a gerontological nurse, turned to a care management company after almost two years of struggling on her own to meet the needs of a widowed father 650 miles away. "I needed someone to find and manage the caregivers," she says. "They did an excellent job of assessing the situation and came up with good candidates for us to interview."

Private care management, which is generally not covered by either Medicare or private insurance, can cost from $60 to $125 an hour, and costs can mount if long-term monitoring of care is needed. But even where money is tight, several hundred dollars for an initial evaluation plus recommendations might be money well spent.

Before you turn to a private care manager, however, you might check with a state or local agency on aging to see what public services exist. In Connecticut, for example, a call to Connecticut Community Care Inc., a private nonprofit agency, can provide one-stop shopping. The agency helped one woman, frantic because

51

her mother was in a nursing home in Florida, transfer her mother to one nearby in Connecticut. An initial evaluation costs $320; time spent in coordinating services and monitoring care is $75 an hour. Because state and federal money provides some of the agency's funding, however, you can place a call for help without first balancing your checkbook. Users may pay privately for services, pay on a sliding scale, or pay through public funds. . . .

Public Policy

If long-term care is provided in the form of a social insurance program like Medicare, the tab is likely to be at least $20 billion a year. Some estimates run to $60 billion. Who's going to pick up the tab? The Catastrophic Coverage Act set a precedent for financing by beneficiaries; it also kicked up a fire storm of protest by older citizens who consider the financing unfair. Proponents of long-term care coverage are faced with the daunting task of devising a way to pay for it that won't generate a similar storm.

But there's a subliminal subtext to the financing issue, centering around how policymakers regard both women and the elderly. Is the country really prepared to replace the unpaid labor of daughters, daughters-in-law, and wives with a paid system of services? Women themselves don't readily relinquish the responsibility. "All the left-over psychological issues surface when a parent is in need," says one daughter, "the whole feeling of should I be doing more." Those feelings can be compounded by cultural taboos; one parent's Cuban heritage, for example, precluded care by anyone but family. Personal feelings aside, as a nation we haven't even managed to pass the Family and Medical Leave Act, which would grant ten weeks of unpaid leave to care for an ill or disabled child or parent; note that spouses aren't included.

Most Americans agree with organizations like OWL that we need support services for caregivers, including widely available respite care, that we need to prevent the impoverishment of the caregiving spouse, and that we need to find some way, as a nation, of paying for long-term care for a rapidly aging population. When asked during the 1988 presidential election whether or not it was "time to consider some kind of government action or insurance program" to support long-term care, registered voters favored government action by nearly 10 to 1.

"All generations have a common stake in maintaining the family as the primary caregiver across the life course."

The Elderly Are a Benefit to Their Children

Eric R. Kingson, Barbara A. Hirshorn, and John M. Cornman

Eric R. Kingson, Barbara A. Hirshorn, and John M. Cornman are the authors of *Ties That Bind: The Interdependence of Generations*. This report was produced by the Gerontological Society of America, a professional organization located in Washington, D.C., whose goal is to support the scientific study of aging. In the following viewpoint, taken from *Ties That Bind*, the authors argue that caring for the elderly is beneficial for families. Such an arrangement enables family members to feel good about helping their elderly relatives and to return the care that the elderly once provided for them.

As you read, consider the following questions:

1. Why do families provide long-term care, according to the authors?
2. What are the benefits of family care for the younger generations, in the author's view?
3. What do the authors claim are the benefits of family care for the elderly?

Eric R. Kingson, Barbara A. Hirshorn and John M. Cornman, *Ties That Bind: The Interdependence of Generations*. Washington, D.C.: Seven Locks Press, 1986. Copyright © The Gerontology Society of America.

Care-giving within the family is the best example of a private intergenerational transfer, for several reasons. The exchange is common, accepted, and preferred; it occurs across the life course; it exemplifies the strong bonds between generations; and it demonstrates the difficulty of measuring intergenerational transfers to determine "inequities."

From birth onward, most individuals will both receive care from and give care to family members, unless disability or illness prevents or hampers them from serving as care-givers. Moreover, families share a wide range of intergenerational relationships and resources (e.g., time, money, thought, sheer physical energy) as part of their care-giving and care-receiving interchange. Thus, although a one-to-one reciprocity between family members is unlikely in either the kind or amount of care given or received, the exchange of care is so common and natural in our lives that we hardly notice much of it taking place unless and until it ceases. To understand the broad spectrum of care provided by families, it is helpful to think in terms of ordinary and extra-ordinary exchanges of care.

Ordinary Family Care-Giving

Regardless of the educational level, socioeconomic status, religion, or ethnic identity of a family's members, many quite ordinary care-giving and care-receiving exchanges occur within the family every day. Some exchanges are short term and discrete, such as tending to a youngster's broken arm; some are of a few years' duration, such as diapering a baby or sending a young person through college; and some last much longer, such as preparing breakfast for one's spouse regularly for most of one's married life. Ordinary exchanges of care can provide both maintenance support—including financial assistance, help with the chores of daily living (baby-sitting, shopping, fixing things in the home), and gift giving—and/or emotional support—including advice on such things as bringing up children or making a major purchase, and expressions of affection, approval, or consolation through visits and telephone conversations. . . .

Extra-Ordinary Family Care-Giving

In addition, many persons will also give and/or receive extra-ordinary care. This might happen, for example, if a child is born with Down's syndrome, if a spouse becomes a paraplegic following an automobile accident, or if an aged parent or grandparent develops a chronic and seriously debilitating heart ailment.

While intergenerational exchanges of extra-ordinary care also take place daily, they are usually responses to support needs that are more demanding than most everyday needs. The opportunity to provide such support is rarely sought after, and when it comes, it quickly and radically alters family life, perhaps for a lifetime.

However, when faced with circumstances requiring extra-ordinary care, the family usually responds as best as it can for as long as it can, for the most part providing both emotional and maintenance support. . . .

For the most part, then, it is primarily the family that is asked to respond when serious support needs arise and, in most cases, to bear most of the on-going costs. Recognizing the support the family usually provides in such circumstances, as well as the innumerable, ordinary care-giving and care-receiving exchanges that take place among family members daily, promotes a better appreciation both of the intergenerational exchanges that take place within families and of the stake *all* generations in our society have in maintaining the family's ability to provide care for its members.

Welcome the Burden

A Roman Catholic theologian, the Reverend James Tunstead Burtchaell, 55, of Notre Dame, insists that a child should welcome the burden of an infirm parent: "We need to be stuck with some people, even sick people. It matures us because it forces us to rearrange our lives, and in doing that we become more generous." In fact most of the elderly *are* cared for at home. Only about 20% of those over 85 are in institutions.

Lee Smith, *Fortune*, March 27, 1989.

We next explore why families are willing to provide extra-ordinary care and some stresses they may encounter when they do. We do so by examining a particular kind of extra-ordinary family care—long-term care of older family members—which may well become a reality for increasing numbers of families at some time during the next several decades.

Older family members in need of long-term care often have both given care to, and received care from, family members over the course of their lives. While some of the approximately 5.2 million older persons with chronic illnesses or disabilities currently living in the community experience only moderate limitations and thus need minimal assistance from family members, those with more severe functional limitations that leave them homebound, and possibly even bedfast, require considerably more assistance. At this point in the course of their lives such individuals are primarily on the receiving end.

The amount and intensity of emotional and maintenance support an elderly family member needs can be substantial. Yet, as when faced with other kinds of extra-ordinary care-giving responsibilities, families usually accept the task and provide the best care they can. The duration of this support may be as long as is necessary, or it may be until the family can no longer provide the requisite skills or financial support or can no longer handle the situation emotionally. At this point, it must turn to outside sources for relief.

Different researchers give a wide range of answers to the question of why families go to the effort—sometimes extreme—of providing this kind of care. . . .

Continuity of Generations

When family members show they care for the survival and quality of life of all generations in a family, including the older ones, they may be reaffirming a sense of family that is more than just a passing on of genetic information and learned behavior, as it is with other animal species. Such caring may reflect a more expanded notion of family life that recognizes the importance of continuity across generations.

This recognition is demonstrated by children and grandchildren *wanting to provide* this care and seeing their older relatives *wanting to receive* it from them. At the same time, these younger generations *learn to want* and *expect* such care in the future from their own children and grandchildren. Thus, there is an expectation that the intergenerational exchange of care will persist over time to preserve not only the continued existence of one particular older family member but also the importance of the older generations to family life.

The concept of care as a resource both given and received over the entire course of life implies a reciprocity between family members. Reciprocity of emotional and maintenance support between *healthy* older family members and members of the other generations in a family is substantial.

However, the pattern of exchange may differ markedly when the older family member requires family support for a chronic illness or disability. In this situation, according to analysts Amy Horowitz and Lois Shindelman:

> Reciprocity is conceptualized as stemming from the "credits"
> earned *by* the older persons for past help given to the caregivers.
> It is an obligation which stems from gratitude and is manifested
> in the desire to repay the older relative for past services rendered.

Thus, an older person needing long-term care may go to family members for support because these are the people the older person helped in the past.

Somewhat related to perceptions of what it means to reciprocate in this intergenerational exchange is the value placed on "filial responsibility." While there is some historical precedent in both Far Eastern and some Western history for filial responsibility toward the old as a tradition, there are two reasons why filial responsibility is fairly new as a major motivation for intergenerational care-giving. First, until the advent of an aging society, relatively few families were faced with the question of providing care for older people. And second, until the end of the nineteenth century, older family members owned the means of production (farms, farm equipment, etc.) until death, which made intergenerational relations more a question of economic survival than of filial responsibility. However, industrialization at the turn of the century took the means of economic survival out of the hands of parents. The decision to take care of elderly family members thus changed from one of necessity to one of choice, and the value of filial responsibility grew in importance as a motivation for intergenerational care-giving. Today it appears to be a strong factor behind family care-giving behavior. For example, in one recent study that explored what three generations of women believe to constitute appropriate filial behavior toward elderly widowed mothers, researchers Elaine Brody, Pauline Johnsen, and Mark Fulcomer report that "large majorities of each generation indicated that adult children—regardless of gender, marital status, or work status—should adjust their family schedules . . . when needed." Elsewhere, Brody further notes:

> At some level of awareness, members of all generations may harbor the expectation that the devotion and care given by the young parent to the infant and child—that total, primordial commitment which is the original paradigm for caregiving to those who are dependent—should be reciprocated and the indebtedness repaid in kind when the parent, having grown old, becomes dependent.

And she points out that although repaying this debt is, of course, an impossible task, many adult children attempt it nevertheless.

Meaningful Contributions

The once-accepted and honorable image of the senior citizen's place in society appears to be blurring amid the culture's apparent rush to worship the idol of youth. Yet this observer says that if we continue to relegate members of the older generation to isolated enclaves, we will be much the poorer.

Have we forgotten their great ability to contribute to more meaningful family lives and social structures?

Miriam Adeney, *Eternity*, June 1987.

Yet perhaps the importance of filial responsibility lies in another experience, a lesson that many people learn in childhood but that may still leave a lifelong imprint, whatever their adherence to organized religion. Quite possibly, when a person sees an elderly individual with support needs, he or she recalls and feels compelled to heed the biblical commandment, "Honor thy father and mother."

Since reciprocity and/or filial responsibility seem central to explaining why families provide long-term care to their elderly relatives, the intergenerational flow of resources may appear to go only to the older person. However, it is important to note that benefits may also flow back to the provider, an exchange which further underscores the concept of interdependence across the life course.

As mentioned previously, individuals with chronic illnesses or disabilities must come to terms with a diminution of their self-reliance, an acceptance which is extremely difficult for most people to reach. However, just as it is essential for the older person needing support to be able to *give up* some self-reliance and *depend* more on other family members, it is equally essential for those other family members to *accept* the older person's increased need for their support. As Brody points out, "not only must the adult child have the capacity to permit the parent to be dependent, but the parent must have the capacity to be appropriately dependent so as to permit the adult child to be dependable."

Part of the importance to family members obviously lies in the fact that they are the providers of this care. Yet it is important for another, very personal reason as well. It is very difficult for most people to come to terms with having to rely on others for extra-ordinary care. The refusal of older relatives to adjust to their diminished autonomy and to their reliance on others for long-term care needs may make the task even more difficult for all concerned. However, by accepting and dealing with older relatives with extra-ordinary needs, the care-giver can learn to appreciate both the difficulty *and* the necessity of adjusting to diminished autonomy. Thus, care-giving to older family members with chronic problems can have a very positive impact on the personal development of care-givers as well.

Stresses to the Family

Long-term care of older family members is similar to other kinds of extra-ordinary care-giving over the life course in that it tests a family's care-giving abilities and requires readjustments in other spheres of family life. Such adjustments often are stressful. In some cases the resulting stresses affect the health and welfare of other family members as well as of the primary provider(s). Generally, however, the closer the relationship to the care-receiver, the greater the strain on the care-giver. Thus spouses, followed by children, tend to be the most stressed.

The ability and willingness of individual families to handle stresses that may result from providing long-term care vary greatly according to individual circumstances, strength of family ties, and the particular reasons behind a family's decision to provide such care. In general, however, the capacity of families to do so in the future may be significantly diminished by several demographic and societal trends that point to changes in *demand* for care, family structures, and living arrangements.

For example, the nation can expect a sharp increase in the number of elderly requiring long-term care. At the same time, the projected increase in single-parent households and the divorce rate may affect the ability of families to provide care, while the increasing number of women entering the work force may leave women, the traditional care-givers, less available and less willing to provide care on a long-term basis. Also as increasing numbers of women have fewer or no children, the supply of future family care-givers may also diminish. . . .

A Common Stake

Even the cursory discussion presented makes clear the great number and variety of intergenerational transfers that occur as the result of care-giving within the family and the strong preference families have for providing these transfers. We have also tried to indicate demographic and societal trends that will increasingly strain the family's ability and willingness to provide such care. At issue are the traditional values of family-provided care, the quality of life for many care-givers and care-receivers alike, and the costs of providing care.

Examined from the viewpoint of the interdependence of generations, all generations have a common stake in maintaining the family as the primary care-giver across the life course, especially as the family's ability to provide such care is coming increasingly under stress. Clearly, a public policy response will be required to help families continue in their traditional care-giving role. That response should be broad enough to recognize the common stake generations have in preserving that role.

Distinguishing Bias From Reason

When dealing with controversial issues, many people allow their feelings to dominate their powers of reason. Thus, one of the most important critical thinking skills is the ability to distinguish between statements based upon emotion or bias and conclusions based upon a rational consideration of the facts.

Many of the following statements are taken from the viewpoints in this chapter. Consider each statement carefully. *Mark R for any statement you believe is based on reason or a rational consideration of the facts. Mark B for any statement you believe is based on bias, prejudice, or emotion. Mark I for any statement you think is impossible to judge.*

If you are doing this activity as a member of a class or group, compare your answers with those of other class or group members. Be able to defend your answers. You may discover that others come to different conclusions than you do. Listening to the rationale others present for their answers may give you valuable insights in distinguishing between bias and reason.

> R = *a statement based upon reason*
> B = *a statement based on bias*
> I = *a statement impossible to judge*

1. Social psychologists say that retirement can be an opportunity for further development as a person because you have more free time to devote to other pursuits besides making a living.

2. A society that does not care for its elder members is very cruel and selfish.

3. A marketing survey showed that most people thought Clara Peller's performance in the Wendy's ads made older people look silly, cranky, and unattractive.

4. Retirement means being exiled from productive society and social involvement.

5. Most retired people have too much empty leisure time on their hands.

6. The statistics show that the aged do not have any political power as a group since they do not all vote alike on the issues.

7. The elderly are betrayed by their bodies, their culture, and their government.

8. Studies show that advertisers have tended to stereotype the elderly.

9. Historically, the age-based organizations have not played an influential role in shaping Medicare, Social Security, and other major programs.

10. If we can get a man to the moon, we ought to be able to get dentures to people who built our society.

11. Just as the baby boomers have transformed society's institutions, as they age, they will demand the expansion of social and economic roles for older people.

12. Getting old means getting weaker and forgetful, and not being much fun.

13. That elderly people are being forced to eat dog food to keep from starving to death is a lot of hogwash.

14. Having interviewed many retired persons about their life-styles leads me to conclude that there are many reasons and motives for retiring.

15. The elderly are an overly pampered group who hoard their money and then demand government entitlements.

Periodical Bibliography

The following articles have been selected to supplement the diverse views presented in this chapter.

Frank Bowe — "Why Seniors Don't Use Technology," *Technology Review*, August/September 1988.

K.C. Cole — "Aging Bull," *Ms.*, April 1989.

Kingsley Davis — "Our Idle Retirees Drag Down the Economy," *The New York Times*, October 18, 1988.

David DeVoss — "Empire of the Old," *Los Angeles Times Magazine*, February 12, 1989.

Elizabeth Ehrlich and Susan B. Garland — "For American Business, a New World of Workers," *Business Week*, September 19, 1988.

Neal B. Freeman — "Old People's Power," *National Review*, December 9, 1988.

Elizabeth Janeway — "Who Says Old?" *World Monitor*, June 1989.

Sheila Kaplan — "The New Generation Gap: The Politics of Generational Justice," *Common Cause Magazine*, March/April 1987.

David Larsen — "Golden Choices," *Los Angeles Times*, October 9, 1989.

Phillip Longman — "The Challenge of an Aging Society," *The Futurist*, September/October 1988.

Dyan Machan — "Cultivating the Gray," *Forbes*, September 4, 1989.

Janet Novack — "Tea, Sympathy and Direct Mail," *Forbes*, September 18, 1989.

Jonathan Peterson and Robert A. Rosenblatt — "'Boomers' Face a Brave Old World," *Los Angeles Times*, December 30, 1986.

Robin Toner — "Congress Feels the Clout of the Angered Elderly," *The New York Times*, July 24, 1989.

Anastasia Toufexis — "Older—But Coming on Strong," *Time*, February 22, 1988.

Are the Elderly Poor?

Chapter Preface

Skyrocketing budget deficits, fear over Japan taking the world economic lead, widespread coverage of financial mismanagement—in newspapers and on television programs across the country, Americans are told that the government must cut back in order to reverse the nation's economic decline. It is this atmosphere that provides the backdrop for a heated and controversial issue: Are the elderly poor?

Spokespeople for the elderly are enraged at the suggestion that the elderly do not need the Social Security and Medicare benefits they receive. These people argue that statistics prove it is the elderly—especially elderly women and minorities—that are the poorest segments of the U.S. population. Society's resources are well spent on the elderly, they maintain, and cutting back would lead to more poverty among this population.

Those who believe the elderly are not poor and do not need as much government aid as they currently receive argue that these resources are desperately needed elsewhere. They cite the many assets the elderly hold, including their own homes, private savings, and a lifetime accumulation of possessions. These critics argue that statistics prove that children are society's poorest members, and it is these children who deserve more federal aid.

The authors in this chapter debate this emotional issue. At the heart of their arguments is the question of how society should apportion its limited resources.

"The fact is that millions of the elderly are poor, and millions more are living in economic circumstances virtually indistinguishable from poverty."

The Elderly Are Poor

Families USA Foundation

Families USA Foundation is a Boston-based organization that funds research on the elderly. The following viewpoint is taken from a Foundation report on the economics of old age. In the report, the authors assert that faulty and unfair reports have made the elderly population appear wealthier than it really is. They believe poverty among the elderly is a genuine problem that deserves attention.

As you read, consider the following questions:

1. What do the authors cite as the most common myths about poverty among the elderly?
2. What changes does Families USA Foundation advocate to reduce the number of poor senior citizens?
3. How has the government helped perpetuate poverty among retired people, according to the authors?

Families USA Foundation, *On the Other Side of Easy Street: Myths About the Economics of Old Age.* Washington, D.C.: Families U.S.A. Foundation, 1987. Reprinted with permission.

MYTH: 'There is little poverty among the elderly.'

In recent years, advocates of a retrenchment in federal programs for the elderly have attempted to demonstrate that older Americans are, as a group, comparatively well off—and that poverty among the elderly has all but disappeared. Generally, this claim is buttressed by references to the most recent Census Bureau data on income and poverty. Any objective analysis should begin by scrutinizing these statistics—because they have been used in misleading ways.

True, some of the elderly are affluent. And more of the elderly are economically secure than was the case a generation ago—a welcome development, and an accomplishment of which our society should be proud. But it's a myth that poverty among the elderly has all but vanished. The fact is that millions of the elderly are poor, and millions more are living in economic circumstances virtually indistinguishable from poverty.

Definition of Poverty

According to the Census Bureau, some 3.456 million elderly Americans (men and women aged 65 or older) were poor in 1985. This was an increase of 126,000 from the year before, and the elderly were the only age group to experience such an increase. Still, when we consider that the total elderly population in 1985 was 27.322 million, the number living in poverty may seem reassuringly low. But it is important to know how that number is calculated—beginning with the basic definition of poverty.

The federal government's definition of poverty, as applied to the elderly, is strict indeed. The official "poverty line" for an elderly individual in 1985 was $5,156. That is, an elderly person living alone was considered poor only if his or her income for the year fell below that level. For an elderly couple, the 1985 poverty line was $6,503.

What do these figures mean in real-life terms? For an individual, they mean that you were not officially poor if your weekly income exceeded $99. The cut-off line for a couple was $125. If your income was greater—even by only a dollar—you were not poor, according to the Census Bureau.

FACT: The official measure of poverty is discriminatorily lower for the elderly than for other age groups.

Anyone's definition of poverty is open to subjective criticism, of course. But the task of objectively assessing the true extent of poverty among the elderly is made more difficult by the existence of an important statistical inconsistency.

The Census Bureau applies a different poverty standard to the elderly than to other adult age groups. In effect, the federal government assumes that an adult 65 years of age or older can escape poverty on less income than an adult 64 or younger.

In the real world, such an assertion would be dismissed as nonsense. But in the world of demographic data, this double standard is widely overlooked—and its tacit acceptance reinforces the inaccurate impression that few of the elderly are poor.

In 1985, the official poverty line for a single adult *younger* than 65 was $5,593—some $437 higher than the $5,156 for an individual 65 or older. The poverty threshold was thus deemed to be 8.5 percent higher for a non-elderly person than for an individual officially defined as elderly. The discriminatory definition is even more striking when applied to couples. Here the differential is 11.2 percent: $7,231 for couples below 65 years of age compared to $6,503 for elderly couples.

This double standard creates conflicting definitions of poverty based solely on age, a discrepancy that makes no sense when applied to real-world circumstances. Take the obvious example. Assume that you are 64 years old, living alone, with an annual income of $5,500. According to the government, you are poor—a contention you doubtless wouldn't dispute. Now, assume that you pass your 65th birthday. You're a year older. Your income has not changed: it is still $5,500. Are you still poor? No, says the government, you are poor no more.

Discriminatory Standards

If the same poverty standard were applied to the elderly as is now used to measure poverty among other age groups, the number of elderly poor would increase by 450,000 to 700,000, jumping from 3.5 million under the current count to as high as 4.2 million. By the same token, the poverty rate for the elderly would increase

POVERTY STATUS BY ADULT AGE GROUP IN 1985

Age Group	Total Number*	Below Poverty Level*	Percent of Total
22-44 years	86,871	9,823	11.3%
45-54 years	22,662	1,911	8.4%
55-59 years	11,212	1,103	9.8%
60-64 years	10,849	1,222	11.3%
65+ years	27,322	3,456-4,156	12.6%-15.2%

*Figures in thousands in 1985

(The lower figure for the 65+ age group reflects the number and percentage of poor persons based on the discriminatory aged poverty line, while the higher figure represents the highest range estimate of poverty based on the non-discriminatory non-aged poverty line.)

Families USA Foundation. Reprinted with permission.

from 12.6 percent (under the current discriminatory standard) to as high as 15.2 percent.

In other words, if a consistent poverty standard were applied to all age groups, the poverty rate for the elderly would be higher than the poverty rate for the overall population.

Why are the elderly subjected to a different definition of poverty? The discrepancy can be traced to a fluke of social history. Poverty definitions used in the United States today were developed in the 1960s, based on the cost of a minimally adequate household food budget—the "Economy Food Plan"—developed by the U.S. Department of Agriculture. Poverty lines were plotted simply by calculating the cost of the food plan for different households and then multiplying by three—because USDA surveys showed that the average family spent a third of its income on food.

When the criteria for the Economy Food Plan were being worked out, analysts assumed that an adequate diet for a typical elderly person would be less costly than for a typical person under 65, because older people in good health have lower nutritional requirements than younger people. If that is so, and if poverty-level income is to be calculated merely by multiplying the food budget by three, then it follows that multiplying a lower food budget by three yields a lower total income needed to escape poverty. This reasoning led to the creation of a lower poverty threshold for the elderly than for other adult age groups.

The Elderly Poor

Some of the assumptions used in developing the Economy Food Plan were badly flawed. (Despite much subsequent criticism, however, they have never been corrected.) First, the food plan was designed to meet the needs of healthy people. But the elderly poor are not necessarily healthy. On the contrary, elderly people—especially those who have lived in or near poverty for much of their adult lives—are more likely than other adults to have serious health problems requiring special diets and nutritional supplements. Unless they are forced by circumstance to neglect such needs, their food costs may be just as high as those of younger people—if not higher. (This can be true for many other reasons, too. For example, many of the elderly poor in cities are forced to rely heavily on small neighborhood stores where prices are generally higher than in suburban supermarkets.)

Second, and most important, no household costs other than food were considered in calculating the poverty line. If these costs were included in the calculation, the number of elderly poor would certainly increase. While the elderly as a group (poor and non-poor combined) may spend less of their total income than the non-elderly on certain expenses (such as housing), they spend *substantially more* than the non-elderly on health care. In fact, the elderly spend more than three times as much of their disposable income on out-of-pocket health care costs as the non-elderly do. But this is not factored into the poverty equation.

Instead, the methodology used to compute the poverty line for the elderly relies on an assumption that, because food costs for healthy elderly people are lower than food costs for healthy younger people, the costs of *all* necessities must therefore be lower for the elderly—healthy or otherwise. Such an assumption is simply not valid.

For these reasons, the official definition of poverty, as used to calculate the total number of elderly poor, is both deficient and discriminatory. It seriously understates the extent of poverty among the elderly.

Elder Poverty

Most elders are not eating steak. In fact, official poverty figures hide the 30% of elders barely out of poverty. Elder poverty persists because if you are poor before you reach 65, you will be poor afterward; if you are a member of the middle class in your younger years, you have a very good chance of being poor during your elder years; if you are rich while you are working, you will be rich when you retire.

Patricia Horn, *Dollars & Sense*, January/February 1988.

FACT: Poverty among the elderly is more widespread than in any other adult age group.

The Census Bureau calculates the incidence of poverty within many different age groupings. The poverty rate among children under 18 is very high: 20.7 percent. And, since children constitute more than a fourth of the total U.S. population, the statistical impact of their exceptionally high poverty rate is obviously great. The population of children under 18 is approximately 63 million (more than twice the size of the elderly population). Nearly two out of every five poor people in the U.S. in 1985 were under 18. That fact drives up the poverty rate for the entire under-65 population.

As a result, the combined poverty rate for adults under 65 and for children under 18 is higher than the poverty rate for the elderly: 14.1 percent for those under 65 versus 12.6 percent (or up to 15.2 percent, if the non-discriminatory standard is used) for the elderly. These numbers reinforce the impression that poverty is lower for the elderly than for the rest of the population.

It should be noted that we do not propose to contribute to an already troublesome intergenerational controversy over the question of which age group suffers more severely. Addressing the poverty rate among children ought to be high on the agenda of any society capable of compassion and concern for the future. At the same time, the extraordinary dimensions of the crisis among children need not cause us to downplay the extent of poverty among adults. And the fact is that, among adults, poverty is more widespread for the elderly than for any other age group. This is true regardless of whether one uses the discriminatory definition of poverty applied only to the elderly or the standard used for all other age groups.

Comparisons among different adult groups become even more significant when we take into account the special economic circumstances affecting them. Consider, for example, the group of adults aged 45 to 54. These are generally the peak income-producing years. In recent years, considerable numbers of men and women within this group have been hard-hit by structural unemployment, which has created a large pool of unemployed middle-aged workers without the skills to find jobs in a changing economy. The poverty rate within this age group as a whole, however, is 8.4 percent—significant to those suffering poverty, but statistically far less severe than the poverty rate of the elderly (12.6 percent rate using the discriminatory poverty line, and up to 15.2 percent using the non-discriminatory poverty line).

FACT: *Poverty is very high among significant groups of the elderly.*
Poverty is an especially widespread and deep-rooted problem for some segments of the elderly population: for minorities, compared to whites; for women, compared to men; for the "oldest old," compared to the rest of the elderly.

The Risk of Being Poor

• Minorities: The risk of being poor is typically two to three times as great for elderly minority-group members as for whites. Older blacks are nearly three times as likely to be poor as elderly whites: 31.5 percent of elderly blacks were poor in 1985, compared to 11 percent of elderly whites. The poverty rate is also extraordinarily high among elderly Hispanics—23.9 percent in 1985.

• Women: Poverty is much more prevalent among elderly women than among elderly men. Women constitute 58.7 percent of the total elderly population, but they account for 72.4 percent of the elderly poor. Elderly women have a poverty rate nearly twice that for men: 15.6 percent of all elderly women were poor in 1985, compared to 8.5 percent of all elderly men. For elderly women living alone, the rate is 26.8 percent. Seven out of ten poor elderly women live alone.

Elderly black women experience a form of "triple jeopardy" because of their age, race, and sex. The poverty rate for elderly black women in 1985 was 34.8 percent, meaning that more than one out of every three was poor. For older black women who live alone, poverty is even more pervasive. An astonishing 54.5 percent of these women were poor in 1985, marking them as among the most severely disadvantaged groups in our society today.

• The 'oldest old': Poverty also takes an especially heavy toll among the "oldest old." About 18.7 percent of all persons 85 years or older are poor. Deprivation is even greater among women in the oldest age groups. The poverty rate for women 85 or older is 19.7 percent. It is worth noting that this rate is about the same as the poverty rate for children under 18. Poverty assaults the youngest and oldest among us—the two groups least able to defend themselves.

FACT: The elderly poor are more likely to suffer long-term poverty.

The elderly have a substantially higher poverty rate than the general population when poverty is measured across time. For the elderly, poverty is likely to be long-term—that is, both persistent and inescapable.

This is *not* the prevailing pattern for the rest of the population. Researchers have found that one out of every four Americans is poor for at least one year in a ten-year period, yet more than half of those so afflicted manage to escape poverty after a year or two—and nearly 90 percent manage to avoid becoming mired in long-term poverty (defined as being poor for at least eight years out of ten).

Persistent Poverty

It's important to keep in mind that escaping poverty is not the same thing as becoming affluent. The "escape" in question may be marginal—crossing a statistical classification line rather than actually becoming comfortable. Nevertheless, the distinction between short-term and long-term poverty is significant. Clearly, it is less overwhelming to be poor in some years and not quite poor in others than to bump along in rockbottom poverty year after year after year. Persistent poverty can lead to the abandonment of hope and, if sufficiently widespread, may create an underclass of people beyond reach of conventional strategies to ameliorate poverty. Those most likely to be persistently poor are blacks, female-headed families, the disabled, and the elderly. . . .

FACT: You can't eliminate poverty by redefining it.

Those who portray the elderly as relatively affluent are inclined to rely on a form of argument that would make poverty go away by redefining it. The poverty rate for the elderly would be greatly reduced, they argue, if non-cash federal benefits (like Medicare, Medicaid, food stamps, and housing subsidies) were counted as income. If this were done, they assert, the poverty rate among the elderly would plummet—to somewhere in the vicinity of 3 percent.

When non-cash benefits are assigned a cash value and included in income calculations, the major impact on the poverty rate comes from counting Medicare and Medicaid. Food stamps and housing aid are provided to only a minority of the elderly, and counting these benefits as income produces only modest changes in the poverty rate for the elderly as a group. But Medicare and Medicaid are broad-ranging programs that account for more than 90 percent of federal expenditures of non-cash benefits for the elderly. When they are counted as income, they can appear to reduce the elderly poverty rate dramatically.

An Illusory Poverty Rate

This appearance is illusory, however. The methodology required to yield a 3-percent poverty rate for the elderly has been overwhelmingly rejected by most of the nation's leading experts on poverty. At a conference sponsored by the Census Bureau in December 1985, some 125 experts met to discuss counting non-cash benefits in measuring poverty. The analysts were divided over whether it is feasible, let alone appropriate, to place a dollar value on Medicare and Medicaid benefits and count them as income. But they agreed that if medical benefits are counted, then the poverty threshold must be recomputed too—and presumably raised.

The current poverty threshold ($5,156 for an elderly individual and $6,503 for an elderly couple in 1985) is based on cash income only. It cannot properly be used to measure poverty if non-cash medical benefits are counted, the experts warned. If Medicare and Medicaid benefits are added to income without adjusting the poverty line, an elderly person could be considered non-poor—on the basis of revised ''total'' income—even if he or she lacked the cash to pay for a minimally adequate diet and other basic necessities. . . .

There may be valid arguments for recalculating income and poverty across the board, for all age groups, using sophisticated methodologies that assign realistic cash values to various non-cash benefits, and recomputing the poverty line. In the meantime, however, poverty among the elderly can't be eliminated simply by redefining it.

"Americans over 65 are the second-richest age group in U.S. society."

The Elderly Are Not Poor

Robert England

The author of the following viewpoint, Robert England, argues that fewer elderly are living below the poverty line than ever before. According to England, federal and state entitlement programs like Social Security now permit the elderly to retain their personal assets and maintain their standard of living. Thus, England argues, it is a myth that the elderly are poor. England is a staff writer for *Insight*, a weekly newsmagazine.

As you read, consider the following questions:

1. How has the elderly population increased its standard of living, according to the author?
2. According to England, how has the Social Security program affected the elderly's financial situation?
3. What does England believe should happen to other social programs designed for the elderly?

Robert England, "Aging in America: Wealth and the Elderly." Reprinted with permission from **Insight**: © 1987 **Insight**. All rights reserved.

Contrary to popular myth, America's senior citizens are not as a general rule eating dog food in squalid apartments in declining, crime-ridden urban neighborhoods as they wait for the Social Security check to arrive.

In fact, Americans over 65 are the second-richest age group in U.S. society. Only those Americans in the next-oldest age bracket, from 55 to 64, are better-off. The assets of the aged are now nearly twice the median for the nation: The median net worth of their households in 1984 was $60,266, while the median for all Americans was $32,677.

And it is not just assets and home equity that makes them wealthier. If one divides household income by the number of members in the household, the elderly earn slightly more than the national average. More significant, the elderly household income is greater than that for households headed by the youngest working Americans, those under 25. Some economists say this marks the reversal of a historical trend: Workers traditionally have earned more money than retirees.

While there are still disadvantaged people among the elderly, those over 65 have since 1982 reported a lower poverty rate than the population as a whole and are widening their advantage—another reversal of historical trends.

Saving into Retirement

Some elderly continue to save into retirement and do not reduce their assets. Even if one removes home equity (the biggest slice of most Americans' wealth), the elderly had a median household net worth of $18,790. The general population: $7,783.

The Federal Reserve Board's Survey of Consumer Finances for 1983 pinpoints the sources of wealth for the elderly: More than half have savings accounts, with a median value of $2,400. Certificates of deposit are held by 37 percent of elderly families, with a median value of $20,000. Stock holdings by 21 percent of the elderly have a median value of $10,000, while money market accounts, held by 18 percent, have a median value of $11,000.

It appears that more of the elderly have also achieved another important goal: Those with Social Security and a pension are more likely to maintain the standard of living they could afford when they worked, according to economist Emily S. Andrews of the Employee Benefit Research Institute. She estimates the total of all pension and Social Security income paid to retirees, government and private, to be $300 billion a year.

Overall, the economist says, "it's a tremendous success story. We have succeeded far more than we thought we would as a society" since government and private efforts sought to reduce the 35 percent poverty levels among the elderly in the 1950s.

What all this means is that the traditional "financial life cycle" of the elderly is being altered. The pattern has been that wealth peaks at the point at which people retire; low expenses and high equity combine to offer many people more financial freedom than they have ever had, the kind of freedom that allows for retirement in the first place. But traditionally, during the course of retirement, that wealth has gradually been spent on living costs and health care, until a point at which most elderly people have declined into poverty. That pattern is now being broken for many.

The new self-sufficiency of the elderly may be the best indicator of their condition. More than 90 percent of the elderly live alone or with their spouse. "This is a good reflection of economic well-being," says political economist Bruce Jacobs of the University of Rochester. He cites polls of the aged by Lou Harris in both 1974 and 1981 that report the elderly feel they are in better shape than the rest of the country believes them to be.

How can this be? A number of factors reduce the cost of living for the elderly. The elderly have lower tax rates. Elderly households are smaller than those of most working people: There are no children. Thus they need less to meet basic needs. They have no commuting costs, and clothing requirements are greatly reduced. Most of the 73 percent who own their homes have paid off the mortgages so they have no monthly payment. Many of the others are more likely to live in subsidized public housing than the rest of the population.

More Income

For the most part the elderly are much better off financially than the average nonelderly family. The former have more assets, fewer liabilities, and in many cases, more income.

Thomas J. Dilorenzo, *Reason*, July 1989.

The elderly are the primary beneficiaries of federal social spending. The portion of the federal budget benefiting the aged has risen from 6 percent to 30 percent since 1960, according to Rita Ricardo-Campbell of the Hoover Institution. Rochester's Jacobs calculates that the elderly received more than 75 percent of the $450 billion in social entitlements (those that are not means-tested) in the 1986 federal budget. He estimates total spending on the aged to be about $350 billion, more than the entire defense budget, more than any other part of the federal budget.

A Living Standard

How much retirement income is needed to sustain a living standard? Paul R. Westbrook, a retirement planner with the New Jersey-based Buck Consultants Inc., says a retiree should have enough pension earnings, interest and dividend income, and Social Security to equal 64 percent of his preretirement income. (This is often referred to as the replacement rate, the rate at which retirement income replaces preretirement income.)

Social Security alone usually cannot maintain a retiree's standard of living. Benefits average only 40 percent of the replacement rate, 27 percent and less for those whose incomes were at the ceiling level for Social Security taxes. The average new beneficiary today is paid $467 a month, or $5,604 a year. The highest payment for new beneficiaries is $792 a month, $9,504 a year. The total income for a working couple now retiring is closer to $900 a month.

Part-time work, savings and pensions can close the gap for those who want to reach the replacement rate. Pensions are the key. Andrews has calculated that 37 percent of retirees with families receive pensions. The average benefit is $5,315 a year, about $100 a week (these are the projected benefits for those recently retired and those about to retire, based on the records of workers aged 55 to 64 in 1982). When added to typical Social Security earnings, these pensions nearly double the average income of retirees. Andrews predicts eventually 71 percent of today's young workers will earn pension income when they retire. (Others worry that savings rates among the young may not be high enough and job changes too frequent to provide the good incomes of current retirees.)

Less Money

One reason retirees can live on less money than the working population is that they pay lower taxes. Social Security, the base income for retirees, is not taxed for most recipients (singles earning less than $25,000 a year and couples earning less than $32,000 a year). For others, no more than half of the benefits are counted toward total taxable income.

Data from an income survey of the Bureau of the Census for 1984 reveals that those over 65 had average household incomes of $18,279—somewhat less than the nation's average household income of $27,464. But if that income is divided by the number of household members, the elderly are a little better-off than the national average per household member—$10,316 to $10,207.

Average per capita household income for those over 65 is higher than for all those under 45—those most likely to have children and, thus, more people per household. For example, per capita income for the 35 to 44 age group was $9,646, while for the 25 to 34 group it was $9,147.

These data show that the distribution of wealth and income has changed dramatically since Social Security was created in 1935, according to Rita Ricardo-Campbell. In those days the aged earned far less than working heads of households. Today "more than half of all adults are paying more in Social Security taxes than in personal income tax," she says. These lower incomes for young workers require both spouses to work, including 70 percent of women in their childbearing years.

Poverty Still Exists

All is not rosy for America's elderly. Ricardo-Campbell found those over 85 "are still the poorest in society." The American Association of Retired Persons is concerned about those who are near poverty. "More than one in five of the elderly," says the association's Judy Shub, "are near or below the poverty line."

Better Off Financially

• America's elderly are now better off financially than the population as a whole.

• Children are now by a wide margin the nation's most impoverished age group.

• Young adults now have a harder time making ends meet and face a far stiffer tax burden than their parents did when they were the same age.

In the new America, the old are being enriched at the expense of the young, the present is being financed with tax money expropriated from the future, and one of the legacies children appear to be inheriting from their parents is a diminished standard of living.

"We may be the first society in history of which it can be said that children are worse off than their parents," observes Democratic Sen. Daniel Patrick Moynihan of New York.

Paul Taylor, *The Washington Post National Weekly Edition*, January 20, 1986.

In 1985, the poverty level for the 65-and-older group as a whole was lower than the national level: The national poverty rate was 14 percent but only 12.6 percent for those 65 and older. But since 8.3 percent of the elderly are also officially classified as "near poverty," that brings the total near or below the poverty line to 20.9 percent, compared with 18.7 percent for the nation.

This elderly poverty, however, may be overstated by official data, according to many economists, because it does not include a whole range of government benefits and other mitigating factors. If their market value were considered part of income, benefits such as food stamps and public housing would lower the poverty rate for the elderly to 10.7 percent (and the nation's rate to 12.5 percent), according to June O'Neill of the U.S. Commission on Civil Rights. And if the market value of all medical benefits given to the elderly are added, she says, the poverty rate for those over 65 could be as low as 2.9 percent (and 9.1 percent for the nation).

The elderly may actually be earning more than they report. There's a "strong likelihood" that some elderly people do not report their full income to the Internal Revenue Service, presumably because they fear it may endanger their Social Security earnings, says Robert J. Myers, former executive director of the National Commission on Social Security Reform.

Myers cites a report by Mindy Upp in the January 1983 Social Security Bulletin which claimed that Social Security and IRS data indicate the elderly were earning more than they told the Bureau of the Census in its surveys. The income was underreported by more than 41 percent, the report claims. The Census Bureau estimates that the general population underreports its income to the bureau by about 10 percent.

The elderly who did not work long enough to earn a reasonable Social Security benefit are for the most part covered by Supplemental Security Income and Medicaid (a means-tested benefit, unlike Medicare). . . .

So far, the U.S. public has not balked at expanding programs for the elderly. Since Social Security is viewed as an insurance program, people "feel they paid for it because they contributed to it," says Jacobs. But "what they are getting back today in the form of Social Security and other benefits is between two and three times as much as what their contributions could have earned if they had been invested in the private sector." He says today's workers are paying for this income transfer with lower net earnings. . . .

Government Spending

Jacobs thinks it is time to ask a few pointed questions about all the government spending on the elderly: "Is it enough? Is it too much? If we spend so much, why do we still have some very poor? Why do we still have some who can't pay their medical bills?" The government, he believes, has simply failed to "target the money to the people who need it most."

"Just as it once was fashionable to depict older Americans as universally poor and powerless, it has now become fashionable to depict them as universally affluent."

The Elderly's Wealth Is Exaggerated

Ronald F. Pollack

Ronald F. Pollack is the executive director of Families USA Foundation, an organization in Boston that supports research on the elderly. In the following viewpoint, Pollack contends that the media have created a dangerous new stereotype by depicting America's elderly as wealthy and greedy. In reality, some of the elderly are poor, many others are lower middle class, and very few are affluent, according to Pollack.

As you read, consider the following questions:

1. How does the author refute the argument that fewer workers are having to support more elderly people?
2. How might defense contractors and insurance companies benefit from the myth that the elderly are excessively wealthy, according to the author?
3. What three factors explain poor media coverage of the elderly, in Pollack's opinion?

Reprinted with permission from the Winter 1989 issue of Media&Values Magazine: "Coming of Age: Media and the Mature Audience," published by the Center for Media and Values, 1962 S. Shenandoah St., Los Angeles, CA 90034.

The handsome young NBC reporter looks intently at the politician he's interviewing and asks: "How difficult is it for someone running for office to speak the truth on issues affecting the elderly?"

Later in the broadcast, the reporter's view of "the truth" becomes clear. He characterizes two presidential aspirants who favor cuts in Social Security as "the only candidates talking frankly about Social Security." Presumably, to NBC reporter Steve Kroft at least, candidates who want to *strengthen* Social Security are being something other than frank and truthful.

During his commentary, Kroft describes the elderly as a powerful "special interest" that "over the years built its power base with a carefully cultivated image of frailty and vulnerability while quietly wielding enough power to shape our weekly paychecks." Meetings of the American Association of Retired Persons (AARP) are "indoctrination" sessions of "the most powerful special interest group in the country."

A New Stereotype

Just as it once was fashionable to depict older Americans as universally poor and powerless, it has now become fashionable to depict them as universally affluent and politically unstoppable. To my mind, the new stereotype is as distorted as the old one, and it is more dangerous.

NBC isn't the only network, and television isn't the only medium, to portray the elderly in these terms. *The New Republic* ran a front-cover cartoon of a phalanx of bug-eyed old folks labelled in bold, 60-point headline type: "GREEDY GEEZERS." The issue featured an article by Henry Fairlie, who wrote of sympathy for the elderly as "misdirected."

And the media are increasingly receptive to the strange notion that there is a generational war going on: "Today's Elderly Vs. Tomorrow's" according to the *San Francisco Chronicle*; "The Coming Conflict As We Soak the Young to Enrich the Old," according to *The Washington Post*; "Age Wars: The Coming Battle Between Young and Old," in the words of *Futurist* magazine.

The New York Times describes Social Security recipients as "the monied classes." And *Forbes* magazine sums it all up in an article on "The Old Folks": "The reality is that they're living well. The trouble is, there are too many of them."

Although several myths about the economic status of our grandparents' age group have recently gained currency, the facts are otherwise. They are worth examining one by one.

No. 1: No More Poverty

According to the most pernicious of these false assumptions, elderly poverty has been wiped out. America's elders are living on Easy Street.

"YOU KNOW SOMETHING, ETHEL, INSTEAD OF WHOOPING IT UP, WE'VE SAVED OUR MONEY SO WE CAN MERELY EXIST!"

ROTHCO ORIGINAL

In actuality, poverty remains a painful fact of life for millions of older Americans, especially older women. With one out of eight older Americans surviving below the official poverty line, more than two out of five of our grandparents are living lives of precarious economic vulnerability. Many of our vulnerable elders scrape by on total incomes under $210 a week. All told, the elderly's reward after decades of hard work is the highest poverty rate of all adult Americans. And despite the picture of Greedy Geezers, only about a quarter of the elderly enjoy even the modest comforts that go with annual incomes over $16,000.

No. 2: War Between the Generations

The media have focused on the drama of a war of "intergenerational equity" between young and old, who are forced to compete for scarce resources. The fact, fortunately, is that the generations are not at each other's throats. In American families, grandchildren and grandparents still care about each other, still feel each others' pain.

A national opinion survey conducted by Daniel Yankelovich for the AARP in 1987 drew a portrait of American families bound closely across generational lines. Young and old agreed that family responsibilities were lifelong—specifically that the parents' responsibility to their children doesn't end when children grow up and move out, and also that grown children have a responsibility for helping to support elderly parents.

In fact, the older respondents were most insistent on the parents' continuing obligation toward their children. Younger participants believed most strongly in the responsibility of children to help their parents.

Ignoring the Importance of Family

To believe a picture of generations at loggerheads, the observer must ignore the centrality of the family in American lives. Only in the abstract can the elderly be anything but Grandma or Grandpa to the young. On this point, network news can learn something about reality from the situation comedies.

The notion that old and young are competing for scarce resources is a canard often perpetrated by lobbyists opposed to government spending for the young as well as the old. The real competition for resources in the 1980s has been between the very rich and the rest of us, regardless of age.

No. 3: The Support Pyramid

According to the new litany, the aging of America and a growing pool of retirees have created a disproportionate burden for a shrinking work force struggling to support more and more dependents.

It's just not true that there are fewer workers or more dependents. What has changed is the age of the dependents: fewer children and more grandparents. In fact, there are more workers to support the community and far fewer children to be educated, fed, clothed and nurtured.

Yes, there are more retirees to draw pensions and Social Security, but that change is less dramatic than the decrease in the number of children to be supported.

No. 4: Not Doing Their Share

Subscribers to the greedy geezers myth like to tell us that the elderly haven't been paying enough in these times of federal budget deficits. You hear this often when television news analysts talk about how to reduce the deficit. But the reality is different. Changes in the Social Security structure beginning in the early '80s, massive increases in Medicare premiums and the cost of uncovered hospital charges have all made deep inroads into older persons' pockets.

Between 1981 and 1989, Medicare premiums have nearly tripled, and so has the cost of hospital charges that Medicare won't pay. Sacrifices? Belt tightening? Our elders have been paying their share and more.

With senior poverty still more prevalent than poverty among

other adults, how did the notion of the wealthy old folks spread so rapidly?

In part, it was a result of an attempt by the media (and some senior groups) to brighten up the image of the elderly by focusing on the healthy and the affluent among them. This was encouraged by advertisers who were marketing to affluent seniors.

But it is clear that this agenda also suits the political purposes of those who, in general, oppose *all* social spending.

More Poverty Among the Elderly

Census Bureau reports and other studies tell us that poverty is still far more widespread among the elderly than among younger adults. And one of the chief reasons is the extraordinarily high medical costs for seniors.

Madeleine Provinzano, *People's Daily World*, April 24, 1987.

Take, for instance, the contributions from major defense contractors such as General Dynamics, TRW, Rockwell and conglomerates such as ITT and US Steel to an organization called Americans for Generational Equity (AGE). These corporations have a lot to gain from shifting the heated national debate over deficit reduction away from two major spending areas, defense contracts and expanded tax giveaways. AGE has been running an "educational campaign" on why Social Security (the program you need to cut if you don't want to lose Pentagon spending or tax giveaways) should be lower. Their arguments are shaped to appeal to generations not yet eligible for Social Security benefits.

As noted by Common Cause, the insurance industry, another AGE supporter, is attracted by the probable boost Social Security reductions would bring.

While groups like AGE suggest that the interests of the undeserving elderly conflict with the interests of the deserving young, their energies seem directed more to cutting social spending for grandma than promoting social spending for her grandchildren.

Coverage of Granny-Bashers

Yet groups like AGE have been successful in getting media attention for their sophisticated granny-bashing.

Why? Let me suggest three key reasons:

1. The media have done an incomplete job of educating themselves about social policy questions that affect the elderly. Although there are some first-rate journalists covering these issues—Susan Spencer of CBS, Bob Rosenblatt of the *Los Angeles Times*, and Jerry Estill of the Associated Press come to mind—it's still possible to get assigned to social policy beats with far less

83

expertise than it takes to get assigned to cover high school football. And far too many editors see the problems of the elderly as too boring or depressing for regular coverage.

2. Once again, the elderly are a victim of the media's constant search for the new, the chic, the trendy. Elderly poverty is old hat. The greedy geezers are new, colorful, and, best of all, visually interesting.

3. Third, there's pack journalism. Once the opponents of social spending have placed one story on how granny is robbing junior's piggy bank, every other assignment editor in town wants the story. Truth and enterprise too often fall behind in the rush to keep up with the pack.

Ultimately, the American media does neither a perfect, nor a perfectly miserable, job of reporting on older Americans. Coverage of the funding needed for long-term care, for example, has been quite good. Coverage of Social Security has been generally less successful.

Better Coverage Is Needed

We have a right to expect better. After all, the American press is the freest and probably the best in the world. As America ages, making the problems of the elderly increasingly central to American families, we have a right to hope for more serious and less naive press attention focusing on facts, not fantasy, and resisting the temptation to pit one group against another.

> *"Our senior citizens aren't poor. In fact, some are quite rich."*

The Elderly's Wealth Is Not Exaggerated

Kenneth Eskey

According to opinion polls, many Americans believe most elderly people live in desperate poverty. Kenneth Eskey argues in the following viewpoint that this belief is inaccurate. According to Eskey, many elderly people have significant personal assets, such as stocks, bonds, and their homes. Thus the money they receive from Social Security in addition to their other income pushes them well above the poverty level, he contends. Eskey has been an economics and education reporter for the Scripps Howard News Service in Washington, D.C. for more than twenty years.

As you read, consider the following questions:

1. Why is the belief that the elderly are poor harmful, according to Eskey?
2. What evidence does the author cite to support his argument that the elderly are politically influential?
3. Why does Eskey argue that journalists are reluctant to criticize the elderly?

Kenneth Eskey, "Most Elderly Americans Aren't Living in Poverty," *Manchester Union Leader*, April 28, 1988. Reprinted with permission of Scripps Howard News Service.

After years of treating Grandma and Grandpa like poor relations who don't have two dimes to rub together, Americans finally
are beginning to get the word:

Our senior citizens aren't poor. In fact, some are quite rich.
Many are wealthier than their children. Most are much wealthier
than their grandchildren.

Yet the myth persists—at least among politicians—that elderly
Americans are either bag ladies roaming the streets, retired
librarians living in dusty attics or men in wheelchairs playing
checkers at the county rest home.

Healthier and Happier

The reality is that millions of older Americans are healthier, happier and far more affluent than any previous generation of retirees.

• While only 20 percent of all households are over 65, they own
40 percent of the nation's personal financial assets.

• Three out of four families over the age of 65 own their homes
and most have paid off their mortgages.

By contrast, the woods are full of young people, single and married, who can't afford to buy a house, can't imagine earning
enough money to send children to college and haven't taken a
vacation since they went to Gooseberry Lake after the high school
prom.

Census figures seem to show that the younger you are, the more
likely you are to be poor.

The poverty rate for persons over 65 has fallen to 12.4 percent,
well below the national average, while the poverty rate for
children under 10 was 22 percent, rising to more than 23 percent
for children under 5.

"We may be the first society in history of which it can be said
that children are worse off than their parents," says Sen. Patrick
Moynihan, D-N.Y.

The problem with statistics and generalizations is that they don't
tell the whole story. All old people aren't rich. Many of us have
an older relative who's old, sick and living on a shoestring.

Nor is it accurate to say that all children are poor.

"Many children are much better off than some of the elderly,"
says Sheldon Danziger, who studies poverty at the University of
Wisconsin. "It is unwise to replace one incorrect fact—that the
elderly are needy—with another—that children are needy."

Still, there's no doubt in Danziger's mind that treating the elderly
as though they were a community of paupers makes no sense at
a time when most are well able to take care of themselves.

Historically, much of the nation's wealth has been devoted to
making life "easier" for the next generation.

What we've seen during the 1980s is a massive transfer of income from the young to the old—much of it in Social Security

taxes, but some of it in the form of huge federal budget deficits.

The deficits are nothing more than a loan from children and grandchildren to parents and grandparents, few of whom will be around to help pay off the enormous debt.

The upshot of this cushion of spendable income is that Americans over 65—and certainly those over 50 and 55—are a much better market for products and services than the perky young consumers who sing and dance their way through television commercials.

Poverty Among Children

In 1970, an elderly person was more likely to be living in poverty than a child. Today, a child is nearly *six times* more likely to be poor than an elderly person.

Paul Taylor, *The Washington Post*, January 5, 1986.

Michael Farmer, executive vice president of Age Wave, a California consulting firm, points out that 80 percent of vacation travel is done by people over 50. They buy more than half the luxury cars.

Yet marketing surveys often stop at age 49.

"It's as if they (corporations) believed that once a person turns 50, he or she doesn't buy anything—which, of course, is totally incorrect," Farmer complains.

Fabian Linden, who conducts research for the Conference Board in New York, argues that older people, including those over 65, are "substantially better off" than widely assumed by advertisers. "The idea that old means poor is one of the great myths of American society," he says.

The Myth of Frugal Elderly

One reason marketers have been so slow to respond to senior citizens is that past generations of retirees, perhaps remembering the Great Depression, have tended to hoard money rather than spend it.

That no longer is true.

Anyone who has visited Naples, Fla., Scottsdale, Ariz., Palm Springs, Calif., or any one of a thousand other places where retirees live on the 16th hole of a golf course, or own a cabin cruiser or a condominium, will tell you that frugality is not in style.

There is, of course, another side to the story. The "old old"— many of them widows in their 80s—are less fortunate financially than most couples in their late 60s.

Many of these women were poor before they were old. Others were wiped out financially by a husband's terminal illness. Often, they fall between the cracks of Supplemental Security Income and other welfare programs. They have no pensions. Social Security may be minimal, perhaps less than $215 a month.

The impoverished old may be a dwindling minority, but they are the horrible examples that lobbyists use to dramatize the need for more benefits, or to resist any slowdown in Social Security.

As a political issue, Social Security has become so untouchable that proposals to tax benefits or to reduce cost-of-living increases are considered foolhardy on Capitol Hill. . . .

Most economists regard Social Security as a pay-as-you-go program. Workers pay taxes so that retirees can receive benefits. In a sense, the young support the old, paying 7.51 percent on the first $45,000 of income this year (matched by the employer) so that 38 million retired and disabled Americans can receive monthly checks.

Many, if not most, workers pay more in Social Security taxes than in federal income taxes. It's a flat tax, meaning low-paid workers pay proportionately more than high-paid workers.

In 1990, the tax rate will jump to 7.65 percent, thereby taking an even larger chunk out of the typical paycheck.

Generous Benefits

Contrary to popular supposition, most retirees get back far more than they ever paid into the Social Security system. The average worker retiring in 1988 will recoup every nickel he paid in 21 months. Even the high earners, those who paid the maximum, will be fully reimbursed in 31 months.

Benefits, while not munificent, are increasingly generous, mostly because they are fully indexed to inflation. A typical retiree with eligible spouse is receiving $883 a month. Couples at the high end of the scale are getting as much as $1,257, more than $15,000 a year.

To a small extent, Social Security benefits are taxable. Half the benefits for single retirees with incomes above $25,000 a year and for retired couples with incomes above $32,000 are taxable.

Politically Unpopular Proposals

A number of economists, led by Federal Reserve Chairman Alan Greenspan, argue that all Social Security benefits should be taxable. Why should a worker earning $20,000 a year be paying more than $1,500 a year in Social Security taxes so that a wealthy retiree can receive half of his benefits tax-free?

The argument may sound logical, but politically it doesn't sell.

Even less popular are proposals by economist Barbara Torrey and others that Medicare money spent on affluent retirees should be taken from their estates when they die.

Mrs. Torrey and Cynthia Taeuber, both of whom work for the Census Bureau, suggested that "perhaps their contribution for their own support should come from their assets" after death.

Don't bet on it. "Nobody liked the idea," Mrs. Torrey reports.

Rep. James Moody, D-Wis., was picketed in Milwaukee for wondering whether the assets of the elderly should be used to help pay for nursing home care.

"It's not fair to spend society's money to preserve assets for someone's children," he contends.

None of these proposals is likely to go very far because the country is growing older (the median age is approaching 33) and senior citizens have political clout. They vote.

Economic Status of the Elderly

On average, senior citizens enjoy higher, after-tax per capita income than do members of any age group under age fifty—a truly astounding figure when one considers that nearly all the elderly have withdrawn from the labor force. Morever, the average net worth of households headed by a person over age sixty-five is more than double that of all households headed by a younger person—and more than ten times the net worth of households headed by a person under age thirty-five.

Phillip Longman, *Born to Pay*, 1987.

By 2000, the number of persons over 80 will have grown by two-thirds from 1984. By 2030, there will be only two workers for each retiree. Currently, there are three.

The fact that 28 million Americans, many of them in their 50s, belong to the politically potent American Association of Retired Persons is reason enough for an aspiring lawmaker to tread softly when dealing with retirees.

If anything, Congress is likely to expand Social Security benefits rather than reduce them.

One example: Social Security Commissioner Dorcas Hardy has been pushing a bill that would permit retirees to earn unlimited amounts of money between the ages of 65 and 70 without losing any portion of their benefits. Under present law, retirees under 70 lose $1 in benefits for every $2 they earn over $8,400 a year.

It is an article of faith among journalists that even the mildest criticism of benefits for the elderly is likely to result in a deluge of angry mail.

Robert Samuelson suggested in a newspaper column that several tax breaks for the elderly be eliminated so that taxes for the working poor might be reduced.

One reader informed Samuelson that he is "an alien life form hatched from a rock."

"I hope you never reach 65," a second letter proclaimed.

"By 1986 the elderly enjoyed an official poverty rate significantly below the national average."

Poverty Among the Elderly Is Overestimated

Peter G. Peterson and Neil Howe

Peter G. Peterson is chairman of The Blackstone Group, an investment banking firm in New York. He was the secretary of commerce in 1972 and has long studied and written about national economic issues. Writer Neil Howe is a senior fellow at the Retirement Policy Institute, a research organization in Washington, D.C. In the following viewpoint, Peterson and Howe contend that government entitlement programs such as Social Security and Medicare are harmful and overfunded. Most elderly people are, in fact, more financially secure than younger people, they maintain. Because the poverty rate is highest among children, they support antipoverty efforts aimed at helping that group.

As you read, consider the following questions:

1. Why do the authors argue that government figures actually overestimate the number of poor elderly people?
2. What specific factors do Peterson and Howe cite that account for the elderly's greater degree of financial security?
3. What do the authors believe is ironic about claims that Social Security is a generational contract?

Peter G. Peterson and Neil Howe, *On Borrowed Time: How the Growth in Entitlement Spending Threatens America's Future.* San Francisco, CA: ICS Press, 1987. Reprinted with permission.

An enormous stream of entitlement payments now flows from the U.S. Treasury at the rate of $50 million per hour. It is a stream that dominates the federal budget. Yet the truth about where it goes and what it does often contradicts widespread assumptions that Americans hold about the proper role of government in allocating resources. Entitlements are not just a problem because Social Security and Medicare—the two largest programs—will inevitably become unaffordable during the course of the next century. Fiscal considerations aside, our entire entitlements system is marked by fundamental inequities in its benefit provisions and a lack of clear consensus about the economic and social goals it should be designed to accomplish.

What then are entitlements? The term *entitlements* usually refers to those benefits—whether in cash or in kind—that the federal government automatically pays to qualified individuals. As a rule, entitlement programs ostensibly contain some strong social welfare dimension, though in the case of Social Security and Medicare this is obscured by the insurance metaphors commonly used to describe payroll taxes and benefits. . . .

The Myth of the Needy Elderly

Because well over half of all federal entitlements flow to the 12 percent of Americans aged sixty-five or over, the notion that most entitlements are dispensed on the basis of need is grounded firmly in the myth that the elderly are, almost by definition, destitute, and thus require substantial cash and in-kind support. To be sure, the massive senior lobbies occasionally reinforce this myth in order to consolidate political support for programs benefiting the elderly. To Washington politicians, the phrase "poor, dependent, and elderly" is repeated so often that the last term almost seems a redundancy. Yet the real strength of this perception lies in its prevalence among all age-groups, even outside Washington. Polls invariably show that most of us think old people are very poor. In 1981, for instance, a Harris Poll found that 65 percent of those under age sixty-five believe that "not having enough money to live on" is a serious problem for most of the elderly, and that 54 percent believe that the elderly are worse off than they were twenty years ago. As time passes, we might expect that the true facts about the economic status of the elderly would begin to eclipse such perceptions. Popular myths die hard, however, and there is no guarantee that this one will perish before it has done permanent damage to our economy.

Just what are the facts about the economic well-being of the elderly? We can begin with the radical disparity between the trends in real cash income for the nonelderly and elderly since 1973. For the nonelderly, real income growth has stagnated; for the elderly, it has remained vigorous. From 1960 to 1980, the official median income for elderly families grew by 28 percent relative to nonelderly families; for elderly individuals living alone it grew by 34 percent. This growth was especially rapid in the mid- and late 1970s, when elderly benefit levels were shooting upward and when nonelderly families were actually losing ground in real dollars. But even since 1980, the trend has continued apace: between 1980 and 1985, the median income for elderly families has gained another 13 percent on nonelderly families. Remarkably, the trend favoring the elderly seems to be occurring at all income levels and for all household types.

Today, as a result, many income measures indicate that the elderly are now better off as a group than the nonelderly. *Per household*, it is true that the reported cash income for the elderly (as measured by the Census Bureau) still averages considerably less than cash income for the nonelderly—about 38 percent less in 1986. But this may not seem all that surprising, since elderly households (very few of which consist of more than a married couple) tend to be considerably smaller than nonelderly households. The typical elderly household consists of 1.8 persons; the typical nonelderly household consists of 2.9 persons. *Per capita*, therefore, the elderly by comparison do much better. In fact, per capita cash income is now for the first time edging higher for Americans over sixty-five years of age. In 1984, the elderly came out on top by 1 or 2 percent ($10,316 versus $10,190).

Reforms Are Needed

Baby boomers must pay an unprecedented share of their income to provide benefits to today's elderly—rich and poor alike. Unless we move toward equitable reform of Social Security and Medicare, this burden will make it all the more difficult for the baby boomers to save up against the near inevitability that these benefits will not be available to them when they retire.

Phillip Longman, *The Futurist*, January/February 1986.

These figures, moreover, refer to pretax income. After subtracting out all forms of taxation (including state, local, and property taxes), the elderly did better still in 1984: $8,886 versus $7,876, or a 13 percent advantage over the nonelderly. The large discrepancy between pre- and post-tax comparisons reflects an equivalent difference between relative tax burdens. Much of the elderly's income is not taxable at all (most cash benefits and a large share of income from private pensions and assets, for example); and much of their income and real estate is taxed more lightly (due to age-based exemptions, outdated property-tax assessment values, and the small share of all elderly income subject to payroll taxes). In 1984 the average tax bill for the elderly amounted to about 14 percent of their income, versus 23 percent of income for the nonelderly. Incredibly, as of 1982 about 57 percent of the elderly paid no individual income taxes at all (compared with 13 percent of the nonelderly population), and over 40 percent of elderly households did not even file income tax returns.

Taxes change the picture quite a bit, but other adjustments change it even more. First, we need to take into account noncash income. For the elderly, this primarily means in-kind public benefits such as Medicare. On average, each American aged sixty-five and over received over $2,500 in in-kind benefits in 1984, while only one-tenth of this amount, or about $250, went to each American aged sixty-four and under. (Many younger workers also receive employer-paid health care and related fringes, but this works out to no more than $450 per capita.) . . .

The Elderly's Assets

Finally, there remains the question of net assets, which, as we all know, can be just as important as income in determining living standards. Consider, for example, a person with zero net worth who makes $20,000 yearly from employment, rents an apartment, and pays interest on student and car loans. Then consider a person making $20,000 yearly in pensions, interest, and dividends, who lives in a paid-off home and is entirely debt-free. They have the same income, but they enjoy very different degrees of economic well-being.

Needless to say, it is the elderly who fall most often into the latter category, quite simply because they are in the dominant wealth-holding age bracket. In 1984, 56 percent of all elderly households had a net worth of at least $50,000; only 7 percent had a zero or negative net worth. By contrast, only 23 percent of households headed by persons under forty-five exceeded the $50,000 mark; and 15 percent had a zero or negative net worth. Much of the difference lies in home ownership. Fully three-quarters of all elderly householders are home owners, of whom 84 percent own their homes free and clear; about half of all householders under age forty-five are home owners, of whom nearly all owe mortgages.

But the difference is also reflected in financial assets, where the elderly's median exceeds that of every other age-group for every type of asset—stocks, bonds, and mutual funds, as well as checking, savings, and money-market accounts. During the 1970s and '80s, reported cash income from financial or real property has been one of the elderly's fastest-growing sources of income. It has risen from 15 percent of total elderly income in 1967 to 28 percent in 1984. The comparable figure for the nonelderly is about 5 percent over age forty and almost nil under age forty.

Persons Living in Poverty by Age-Group, 1986

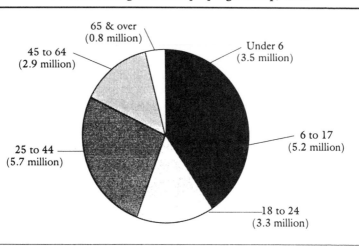

65 & over
(0.8 million)

45 to 64
(2.9 million)

Under 6
(3.5 million)

6 to 17
(5.2 million)

25 to 44
(5.7 million)

18 to 24
(3.3 million)

Based on self-reported cash income *plus* public in-kind benefits such as Medicare, Food Stamps, and rental subsidies. Source: Census Bureau, Current Population Reports.

Given so many different perspectives on comparative affluence, it may be impossible to quantify the relative economic status of the elderly with precision. Weighing all the evidence, however, it is also impossible to defend the claim that on average the elderly are in greater financial need than younger age-groups. Their after-tax income is significantly higher on a per capita basis; after adjustment for noncash benefits and underreporting, it is no doubt higher on a per-household basis; and the high net worth typical of elderly households affords a measure of financial security generally unknown among younger households. . . .

To assess how the elderly are doing, perhaps in the end we can do no better than to ask them directly and return to the Harris Poll mentioned earlier. Interestingly enough, the same poll showing that two-thirds of Americans under sixty-five believe the elderly are destitute also showed that most elderly themselves view their own condition very differently. *In fact, only 17 percent of the elderly respondents regarded low income as a serious problem for them personally, and 58 percent thought it was hardly any problem at all.* Only 1 in 10 elderly respondents agreed that "I can't make ends meet with the income I have now," while 1 in 8 of the nonelderly respondents agreed with this statement. . . .

Nowadays it is a cardinal rule among gerontologists and other experts on aging never to say the elderly are . . . *anything*. The elderly, argue the professionals, are a collection of 27 million individuals so diverse in their income, assets, age, health, prior career experiences, and family relations that any statement true about some of them will be dead wrong about the rest. This diversity, in turn, is often cited to imply that "averages" or "medians" say little about how many elderly need government assistance, or how much assistance is appropriate.

The claim that the elderly are heterogeneous is of course accurate. . . . Many experts have cited such diversity to try to conjure up an image of the elderly divided, like Czarist Russia, into one half living in high-life affluence and the other living in desperate penury. After all, this imagery can be used as one more argument to justify our current system of entitlements.

The Real Picture

The real picture is quite different. To begin with, the greater income spread shows up only in the cash income received by the richest and poorest quarters of the elderly population. The middle half of all elderly households is just as tightly packed around the median income as the middle half of nonelderly households. More important, the poorest quarter of elderly households, while generally lying further beneath the median than younger households, does not extend disproportionately to the very lowest income brackets. As a result, the nearly universal rise in the relative income of the elderly over the past twenty-five years has led to a commensurate decline in their relative incidence of poverty. In 1970 the poverty rate for Americans sixty-five and over (24.6 percent) was still double the rate for younger Americans (11.3 percent). But in 1982, for the first time since poverty rates have been measured, the elderly's rate dipped slightly below the national average. Today it is still dropping, even though the overall poverty rate for all age-groups has been climbing during the 1980s. *By 1986 the elderly enjoyed an official poverty rate significantly below the national average: 12.4 percent, versus 13.8 percent for all persons under sixty-five.* It is still slightly higher than the poverty rate for most younger adults, but well below the rate for the 15-24 age bracket (16.0 percent) and only slightly more than half the rate for children under age 14 (21.2 percent).

It is ludicrous to claim that our existing system of age-based entitlements constitutes a systematic attempt to relieve genuine poverty among the elderly. Consider that in 1986 we spent $270 billion, at the federal level alone, on benefits to the elderly. Yet with only an additional $4 billion, properly targeted, we could raise every elderly household over the poverty level, and with another $4 billion (including, perhaps state and local aid), we could go very far in alleviating the isolation, chronic health problems, and general hardship afflicting many of the near-poor elderly. The tragedy, unfortunately, is that there is no political pressure to enact such patently desirable assistance. And even if there were, we could not afford it, precisely because we cannot presently afford the untargeted assistance we are handing out to middle- and upper-income Americans in such large dollops. . . .

Resenting the Elderly

No group in our society will escape resentment, much less receive veneration and respect, so long as its members are universally subsidized while at the same time many proudly proclaim their ability, if not their proclivity, to continue contributing to society. The fact that age-based entitlement programs are financed by payroll taxes that disproportionately burden the poor when they are young while promising the needy inadequate benefits when they are old compounds the tension. . . . We need a wholly new conception of what it means to grow old in America—one that will bring the elderly as a whole back into the mainstream of society and simultaneously afford dignity and adequate support to those in need.

Phillip Longman, *Born to Pay*, 1987.

In conclusion, we should reemphasize that Social Security is indeed social insurance financed through intergenerational transfers—nothing more and nothing less. It is perfectly legitimate for Americans to make an informed decision to achieve public goals through such a program and to mandate that all citizens must be participants. It is not legitimate to consider Social Security an inviolable contract, exempt from the democratic process that governs all of our other public decisions about how we allocate our national resources.

A tragic irony in the myth of the "generational contract" or "compact" is that its application is so partial and one-sided. When it comes to immediate benefits for a small body of mature voters, we find that appeals to such a contract are both loud and popular. But when it comes to delayed benefits to the potentially infinite number of those unborn or too young to vote, we wait in vain to hear reference to any reciprocal obligation. Where is the congressional leader who reminds us of what we owe to posterity? Who quotes the terms of the contract that guarantees to our children an effective educational system, the rebuilding of our decaying roads and bridges, the preservation of our natural environment, or the technological breakthroughs in the next century with which future working families will compete in the world economy? Such issues, of course, do not only raise questions about the equity of the Social Security "contract"; they also point directly back to the question of its economic sustainability.

"Efforts to pit young against old in a misguided battle for 'generational equity' threaten to imperil not only the interests of the old, but of the society at large."

Poverty Among the Elderly Is Underestimated

Meredith Minkler

In the following viewpoint, Meredith Minkler argues that portraying the elderly as a wealthy, monolithic bloc is both inaccurate and dangerous. According to Minkler, black and Hispanic senior citizens have high rates of poverty. Furthermore, high health care costs often push elderly people toward poverty. Minkler supports more government aid for all impoverished people, young and old. He is an associate professor at the School of Public Health at the University of California at Berkeley.

As you read, consider the following questions:

1. Why does Minkler believe the government's poverty statistics actually underestimate the number of impoverished elderly people?
2. What makes Social Security a popular program among taxpayers, according to the author?
3. Why does the author contend that it is inaccurate to blame government spending on the elderly for U.S. economic problems?

Meredith Minkler, ''The Politics of Generational Equity,'' *SOCIAL POLICY*, Winter 1987. Published by Social Policy Corporation, New York, New York 10036. Copyright 1987 by Social Policy Corporation.

Warning that we "soak the young to enrich the rich," a lead article in the *Washington Post* served to dramatize a growing mass media phenomenon: the reconstruction of our stereotypic views of the elderly—from a poor, impotent, and deserving population subgroup to a wealthy and powerful voting bloc for whom costly government programs flourish at the expense of needy children and financially strapped workers. Editorials railing against the "Social Security ripoff" and a spate of articles in sources ranging from *Reader's Digest* to *Scientific American* proclaim that we've mortgaged our children's future on behalf of an elderly generation unprecedented in wealth and in the disproportionate share of the federal budget that it commands.

Americans for Generational Equity

The alarm has both spawned and been spawned by a fledgling would-be national movement, Americans for Generational Equity (AGE). Born in 1985 under the leadership of Senator David F. Durenberger (R-MN) and Representative James R. Jones (D-OK), AGE defines itself as a nonpartisan, nonprofit coalition whose mission is to build an intellectual and grassroots movement to promote the interest of the younger and future generations in the national political process. Its ambitious objectives include increasing voter participation by younger Americans, dramatically reducing federal budget deficits, reforming Social Security and Medicare, and increasing governmental commitment to environmental concerns and maintenance of the public infrastructure for future generations. Arguing that the young have not had a cause to rally around since the Vietnam War, AGE spokespersons suggest that the fight for generational equity may be just the issue needed to mobilize the 76-million-strong baby-boom generation, born between 1946 and 1964, and whose oldest members are just turning forty. . . .

At the core of AGE's popularity with the media lies its ability to capitalize on growing societal concern over certain facts of life that have coincided with the graying of America. These include:
• a massive federal deficit, amounting to $200 billion a year;
• alarming increases in poverty rates among children, with one in four preschoolers now living in poverty; and
• a 76-million-strong baby-boom generation whose real incomes have declined 19 percent between 1972 and 1987.

These statistics have been coupled with another set of facts and figures used to suggest that the growing elderly population is itself part of the problem. Beginning with the 1985 assertion of the President's Council of Economic Advisors that the elderly are "no longer a disadvantaged group," these findings state that:
• America's elderly are financially better off than the population as a whole;

• the elderly, while representing only 11½ percent of the population, consume 28 percent of the national budget and fully 51 percent of all government expenditures for social services;

• since 1970, Social Security benefits have increased 46 percent in real terms, while inflation-adjusted wages for the rest of the population have declined by 7 percent.

The picture presented is one of a host of societal economic difficulties "caused," in part, by a system of rewards that disproportionately benefits the elderly regardless of their financial status. Congressional policies, under pressure from a powerful gray lobby, are seen as creating a situation in which "today's affluent seniors are unfairly competing for the resources of the future elderly," while Social Security remains "the 'third rail' of American politics," [according to P. Hewitt of AGE].

The Benefits of Social Security

Without Social Security, the poverty rate among seniors would nearly quadruple and the elderly would have to turn for help to their children or other relatives, or to welfare and private charities.

Madeleine Provinzano, *People's Daily World*, April 24, 1987.

The logic behind the message of Americans for Generational Equity is flawed on several counts, each of which will be discussed separately. . . .

Basic to the concept of generational equity is the notion that elderly Americans are, as a group, financially secure. Borrowing statistics from the President's Council of Economic Advisors, proponents of this viewpoint argue that the 1984 poverty rate for elderly Americans was only 12.4 percent (compared to 14.4 percent for younger Americans), and dropped to just 4 percent if the value of Medicare and other in-kind benefits was taken into account. While the economic condition of the elderly as a whole has improved significantly in recent years, these optimistic figures obscure several important realities. First, there is tremendous income variation within the elderly cohort, and deep pockets of poverty continue to exist. According to the 1980 census, for example, fully one-half of all older women had incomes below $5,000, and elderly Black women had a median income of only $3,500. Black elders as a whole had a poverty rate of 39 percent in 1981 by the government's own conservative estimate, and 25.7 percent of Hispanic elders lived in poverty.

Minority elders and the "oldest old," aged 85 and above, not only have extremely high rates of poverty, but also comprise the fastest growing segments of the elderly population. Thus, while only about 8 percent of Blacks are aged 65+, compared to over 12 percent of whites, the Black elderly population has been growing at a rate double that of the white aged group. The number of Black elders further is increasing at twice the rate of the younger Black population. In a similar fashion, the "oldest old" in America are expected to double in number by the turn of the century—from 2½ million today to some 5 million in just 13 years. The very high rates of poverty in the current generation of "old old" may reflect in part a Depression-era cohort effect. At the same time, however, the heavy concentration of women in the 85+ age group, coupled with continued high divorce rates and pay and pension inequities, suggest a significant continuing poverty pocket as the elderly population continue to age.

The myth of a homogenized and financially secure elderly population, in short, breaks down when the figures are disaggregated and the diversity of the elderly is taken into account.

Inadequacy of Poverty Calculations

Analyses that stress the low poverty rates of the aged are misleading on several other counts. First, as Villers Foundation [now Families USA Foundation] director Ron Pollack has noted, comparisons that stress the favorable economic status of the aged vis-à-vis younger cohorts fail to acknowledge the use of two separate poverty lines in the United States—one for those 65 and above and the other for all other age groups. The 1984 poverty line for people under 65 thus was $5,400—fully 8.5 percent higher than the $4,979 poverty line used for the elderly. If the same poverty cutoff had been used for both groups, 15.4 percent of the elderly would have fallen below the line, giving the aged a higher poverty rate than any other age group except children. The inadequacy of even the higher poverty index also merits attention. It is telling, for example, that Molly Orshanksy, the original developer of the poverty index, dismissed it some years ago as failing to accurately account for inflation. By her revised estimates, the number of elderly persons living in or near poverty almost doubles.

Discussions of the role of Social Security and other in-kind transfers in lifting the elderly out of poverty also are problematic. Arthur Blaustein, former chair of the National Advisory Council on Economic Opportunity, has argued that Social Security and other governmental transfers, for the most part, succeeded in "lifting" elders only from a few hundred dollars below the poverty line to a few hundred dollars above it. Indeed, some 11.3 million elders, or 42.6 percent of the elderly, live below 200 percent of the poverty line, which for a person living alone is under $10,000 per year. If a nondiscriminatory poverty line is employed (i.e., if the same poverty yardstick is used for all age groups), approximately 45 percent of the aged have incomes of less than 200 percent of poverty compared to 34.6 percent of other age groups.

Government attempts to reduce poverty by redefining it also bear careful scrutiny in an effort to uncover the true financial status of the elderly and other groups. The argument that poverty in the aged drops to 4 percent when Medicaid and other in-kind transfers are taken into account thus is extremely misleading. By such logic, an elderly woman earning less than $5,000 per year may be counted as being above the poverty line if she is hit by a truck and has $3,000 in hospitalization costs paid for by Medicaid. The fact that she sees none of this $3,000 and probably incurs additional out-of-pocket health-care costs in the form of prescription drugs and other deductibles is ignored in such spurious calculations.

The continuing high health-care costs of the elderly are themselves cause for concern in any attempt to accurately assess the income adequacy of the elderly. Even excluding costly long-term care, for example, the elderly's out-of-pocket health-care costs today are over $1,000 per year—3½ times higher than that of other age groups, and higher proportionately than the amount they spent prior to the enactment of Medicare and Medicaid more than two decades ago. Contrary to popular myth, Medicare pays only about 45 percent of the elderly's medical-care bills, and recipients experienced huge increases in cost sharing (e.g., a 141 percent in-

Don Wright © 1980. Reprinted with permission.

crease in the Part A deductible) under the Reagan Administration. Inflation in health care at a rate roughly double that of the consumer price index further suggests that the *de facto* income adequacy of many elderly may be significantly less than the crude figures imply.

Another criticism of the logic behind intergenerational equity lies in its assumption that the elderly alone have a stake in Social Security, Medicare, and other government programs that are framed as serving only the aged. Arguing that the nation's future "has been sold to the highest bidder among pressure groups and special interests," AGE casts Social Security and other income transfers to the aged in a narrow and simplistic light. Even if one disregards the direct benefits of Social Security to nonelderly segments of the society, e.g., through survivors benefits that reached some 10.4 million persons under age 65 in 1984, the indirect crossgenerational benefits of the program are significant. By providing for the financial needs of the elderly, Social Security thus frees adult children from the need to provide such support directly. As such, it may reduce interfamilial tensions while increasing the dignity of elderly family members who receive benefits. It has been suggested that the family is not perceived by any of the major ethnic groups in America as having major responsibility for meeting the basic material needs of the elderly. Rather, families are able to provide the support they do in part because of the availability of government programs like Social Security. When these programs are cut back, the family's ability to respond may be overtaxed, to the detriment of young and old alike.

Taxpayers Support Social Security

Contrary to recent media claims, there has been little outcry from taxpayers to date about the high costs of Social Security and Medicare. While many factors help explain this phenomenon, not insignificant among them is the fact that younger people in the work force continue to prefer to have their parents indirectly supported than to shoulder this burden themselves in a more direct way. Additionally, of course, today's workers hope to one day be the beneficiaries of these programs. Indeed, even dire predictions that the younger generation will receive, on the average, less than $1 for every dollar paid into Social Security—compared to about $3 on the dollar received by current beneficiaries—appear not to have changed the fact that younger Americans both desire and expect some measure of Social Security and Medicare benefits in their old age.

The reality, in short, stands in sharp contrast to the rhetoric that claims that Social Security is "nothing less than a massive transfer of wealth from the young, many of them struggling, to the elderly, many living comfortably," [as M. Schiffres writes]. Instead, the program is one in which all generations have a stake, and from which all may be seen to profit. . . .

The scapegoating of the elderly as a primary cause of the fiscal crisis has deflected attention from the more compelling and deep-seated causes of the current economic crisis. At the same time, and wittingly or unwittingly fueled by mass media and groups like AGE, it has been used as a political tool to stoke resentment of the elderly and to create perceptions of a forced competition of the aged and younger members of society for limited resources. . . .

While working to improve programs like Social Security is important, such efforts must not detract from the far greater need to work for the strengthening of Social Security, public education, food stamps, Medicaid, AFDC [Aid to Families with Dependent Children], and all of those programs and policies that function in part to meet basic human needs. Ultimately, as Pollack has argued, the central issue is not one of intergenerational equity, but of income equity. Cast in this light, disgracefully inadequate AFDC payments and threatened cuts in Social Security COLAs [cost-of-living allowances], which would plunge millions of elderly persons into poverty, are part of the same problem. Programs and policies "for the elderly" like education and health and social services "for youth" must be redefined as being in fact not "for" these particular subgroups at all, but for society as a whole. As such, and reflecting an appreciation of our interdependence, we should see school bond issues routinely supported by the elderly, improved Medicare coverage endorsed by the young, and a society outraged over the fact that one in four of its children now lives in poverty.

This kind of collective vision is critical, for, in the words of Paul Berry, "if we don't know we are a community, we can't know our losses." To the extent that Americans for Generational Equity have reminded us of the need to look beyond the present to the needs of younger generations and those as yet unborn, they have played an important role in raising national consciousness concerning our essential interdependence. By highlighting in particular the high rates of poverty among our children, they have forced national attention on an American tragedy that demands our collective concern and action.

A Misguided Battle

At the same time, however, by aggregating the elderly and portraying them as a wealthy monolithic bloc profiting at the expense of the young, they have done us a serious disservice. Current efforts to pit young against old in a misguided battle for "generational equity" threaten to imperil not only the interests of the old, but of the society at large.

103

"Instead of trying to destroy the very social insurance programs that have rescued millions of elderly from poverty and hunger, we ought to be expanding them."

Society Should Do More for the Elderly

William R. Hutton

William R. Hutton is the executive director of the National Council of Senior Citizens, a large senior citizens organization in Washington, D.C. that supports programs to help the elderly, including Medicare, Social Security, housing, education, and recreational programs. In the following viewpoint, Hutton argues that social programs for the elderly have succeeded in raising the majority of elderly people above the poverty line. He advocates continuing and increasing programs like Social Security and Medicare to maintain and improve the lives of the elderly.

As you read, consider the following questions:

1. According to Hutton, what common interests do senior citizens and younger people share?
2. What beliefs about the relationship between the elderly and other generations does the author dispute?
3. What public policies does Hutton promote for the elderly?

William R. Hutton, "The Young and the Old Are Not Enemies." Reprinted from USA TODAY MAGAZINE, March 1989. Copyright 1989 by the Society for the Advancement of Education.

One of the more prevalent notions being circulated these days in Washington and around the country is that there is an "intergenerational crisis" brewing between young and old. Under the misleading rubric of Americans for Generational Equity (AGE), a new pressure group, which was created by Sen. David Durenberger (R.-Minn.) and has been called "granny-bashers" and the "yuppie lobby," is framing public-policy questions as if there were competition among the generations.

Economic Hardship

A combination of events—improved economic status of the elderly, rising child poverty, and a baby-boom generation reaching adulthood during a period of relative economic hardship and huge Federal deficits—has led some to conclude erroneously that our society is bankrupting younger generations by spending excessively on the elderly.

Although these critics claim to be working for increased fairness and cooperation between the generations, they promote divisiveness, not equity. Their solution to the problem of poverty among the young is to attack programs that help the old. This strategy is fatally flawed and poses a danger to needy citizens of all ages. In fact, although most major polls and studies indicate little evidence of conflict between age groups, the work of these intergenerational "reformers" well might make such conflict a self-fulfilling prophecy.

The danger of groups like AGE stems from the short-range, myopic approach they take to questions of intergenerational links and benefits—questions which must be examined over time. The distortions arising from this faulty examination, in conjunction with a misguided approach to budgetary questions, has led them to a series of factual errors and misconceptions which they do their best to proliferate. The facts are these:

• The old and the young are not enemies. In fact, their common bonds and needs are much greater than their differences.

• There has been a very significant misrepresentation and deception about the wealth and economic security of the aged. Older Americans are not a group of affluent idlers taking money out of the pockets of younger workers and women and children on welfare. The essential word that should be used when describing the older American population today is "diversity."

• Cutting government assistance to one group does not automatically help another—and, more than likely, will *hurt* both.

• Social Security and other senior assistance programs provide tangible economic returns to all society, young and old.

• All generations share a common stake in the social policies of our nation. Pitting one against the other is where the real danger lies.

While some tensions between various groups in society is natural, the bonds between "old" and "young" are strong, with little evidence of significant intergenerational conflict. In fact, these two groups have more in common than many people are aware of, not the least of which is the shared distinction—albeit a dubious one—of the highest poverty rates of any age group.

A Vulnerable Stage of Life

Over the past 200 years, the U.S. economy has made old age a vulnerable stage of life for most Americans. Few people have sufficient private savings or property income to live comfortably. Economic changes have cut older people off from decent jobs, weakening the allegiance and diminishing the resources of their children. Government attempts to fill even part of the gap are unequally distributed, subject to political battles, and, in most cases, inadequate. The bottom line is that 13% of elders are in poverty and another 29% struggle on incomes within $5,000 of the official poverty line.

Dollars & Sense, January/February 1988.

Because they are the two segments of our population with the greatest need, both have a vested interest in maintaining a strong Federal role in government assistance programs in areas as diverse as education, retirement security, poverty, malnutrition, and Alzheimer's disease. As Nobel laureate economist James Tobin recently wrote, "The history of needs-tested welfare programs shows that their clients, lacking political clout, fared badly in terms of budget austerity and conservative ideology." As such, the young and old are natural compatriots.

This is not to suggest that the elderly's interests are identical to that of children, or that the two groups are never in conflict over the division of scarce human service dollars. However, in the long run, the elderly, as a group, have much more to gain than lose by supporting children's policies and programs.

Critics of older American assistance programs are quick to point out examples of the elderly voting against raising taxes for salary increases for teachers and in favor of politicians who favor laws prohibiting persons under age 50 from living in particular neighborhoods. However, as Eric Kingson points out in his recent book, *Ties that Bind*, care should be taken not to conclude that this is the rule or that the elderly are a cohesive political group intent on enforcing their will against the interests of the young. In fact, recent studies have shown that the voting behavior of the aged appears relatively stable and not susceptible to being changed substantially by age-based appeals.

Lastly, it is important to note that children and the elderly share a strong interest in being treated with dignity when receiving services and benefits to which they are entitled. It is with this understanding that senior citizens' organizations have worked successfully for years with advocates of the family and children to achieve better living standards for needy citizens of *all* ages. However, lobbyists for so-called "intergenerational equity" can upset this balance and cooperation in one fell swoop.

As a start then, it is clear that the framing of issues in terms of competition and conflict between generations is based on a misunderstanding and misrepresentation of relations between them which distract attention from more important ways of examining social issues. At its worst, this concept can be used to justify and build political support for attacks on policies and reductions in social programs that benefit all age groups.

As former Health, Education, and Welfare Secretary Arthur Flemming pointed out: "Many groups prefer to make scapegoats of the nation's grandparents. These groups have an ideological bias against government programs that meet human needs and a fundamental aversion to taxes."

Distributing Resources

Another argument used by these groups to reduce funding for senior programs is the claim that, without "unnecessary" spending on seniors, more money could be going to programs devoted to youth. What this simple-minded strategy ignores is that the redistribution of resources between generations does not guarantee fair treatment or, for that matter, even the minimum standards of care, for poor citizens of any age.

As Kingson points out, "While there is a certain intuitive appeal to equating 'equity' with 'numerical equality,' they are not the same. Such a definition of equity is far too mechanical and narrow. It assumes that the relative needs of children and the elderly for public expenditures are identical and that equal expenditures are the equivalent of social justice."

He also notes that, even if we could agree upon what constitutes a fair distribution of resources among "generations" and achieve such a balance, there is no reason to believe that this definition of social justice would conform with more than a small minority of citizens' views of how society ought to distribute scarce resources.

Clearly, our society should be doing more to address the shameful growth of poverty among children. Yet, we should not fall victim to the trick of pitting one generation against the other for funds in a mythical competition to see who is worse off. There is no doubt that millions of children lack proper food, housing, and education. However, these problems require our attention because of the importance of responding to the needs of children, particularly those children who are at greatest risk—not because "the elderly," or any other group for that matter, are doing better or worse than children.

We also must realize that Social Security and Medicare are not responsible for the poverty of children, nor are any of the other assistance programs that have helped the elderly, as a study by the nonpartisan Congressional Budget Office makes clear. Social programs assisting the young have been gutted, the study shows, as the direct result of enormously rising defense spending since 1983 and of tax loopholes.

In addition, even though senior citizens are in better financial shape than they were 10 or 20 years ago, thanks, in large part, to these insurance programs, there are still large pockets of poverty among the elderly, particularly among Hispanics, blacks, and older women. Moreover, because discriminatingly lower indexes of poverty are used for the elderly and the large number of near-poor who are just over the poverty line is ignored, the myth of a wealthy older generation is perpetrated further.

Many of these myths are due to a failure to recognize the diversity that exists among the elderly. Formerly, the stereotype of the elderly was that of a homogeneous, weak, ill, and poor population. However, the "intergenerational equity" framework draws very heavily on a stereotype of an equally homogeneous population—that of an affluent special-interest group whose very success in gaining entitlements may place an unfair burden on the workforce, especially as the number of older persons increases. Neither stereotype accurately represents the elderly.

Copyright 1982 by Nicole Hollander. Reprinted with permission.

Likewise, simply because some people may fit a stereotype does not mean that the entire characterization is accurate, nor that it is a reason to alter policy. As economist Marilyn Moon of the Urban Institute has noted: "The fact that some elderly are doing well does not imply that government aid should be cut. In fact, part of the significance of the 'good' news is that it underscores the importance of government transfers in achieving gains." If AGE and others truly advocated helping the needy, they would expand, rather than slash, those public-assistance programs that have proven to be both helpful and cost-effective.

Common Responsibilities

Perhaps the greatest danger posed by AGE and others is that they encourage us to shirk the common social responsibilities inherent in our social policies and responsible for our social progress, as well as to ignore a history of respect for the compact of mutual responsibility between generations. In our highly interdependent society, it is both normal and expected that individuals experience personal needs that only other individuals and social institutions can meet. Franklin Roosevelt realized this over 50 years ago, relating social insurance to what he identified as the "hazards and vicissitudes of life."

We prevent economic insecurity through sharing risks very few of us could protect against on our own. To achieve this, social insurance programs like Social Security and Medicare must provide a floor of protection through special provisions for low-wage workers and for certain family members—provisions which, unlike private insurance, make it impossible to turn away prospective participants on the grounds that they are "bad risks."

While there is no guarantee to members of any given generation that they will receive more than they will give, without these public and private intergenerational transfers, the very continuity and progress of society and families would cease. As James Tobin recently wrote, "Total lifetime resources are the relevant measure. . . . A system like [Social Security] is an intergenerational compact: each generation supports its elders with the understanding that the next generation will do the same. Generations who choose not to have children will not have grandchildren to support them in old age, but they can scarcely blame their own parents and grandparents." Although the rate of return can not be guaranteed to be equal or identical, more importantly, the rate of security is.

Public programs for the elderly typically are presented as a one-way flow, benefiting only the elderly. It has become common for analysts and the press to identify the amount of the Federal budget which "goes" to the elderly—again, as if it is only the elderly who have a stake in the benefits provided by these programs. This is both foolish and untrue, just as it is equally foolish to say that only children benefit from programs designed primarily to respond to their needs.

At any one time, it appears that the distribution of benefits and costs from Social Security is "unfair"—with the current young mostly paying and the current elderly mostly taking. Over time, however, individuals clearly are involved in both paying for and benefiting from Social Security.

What is often ignored by critics of Social Security and other senior assistance programs is that these programs provide tangible economic returns for *all* members of society, regardless of age. For instance, if Social Security did not exist, poverty rates among the elderly would increase from 15% to about 50%. Millions more would suffer very significant reductions in their standard of living. Add to this the increased burden of hospital and other medical expenses, and it is clear that the elderly and the other beneficiaries of these programs would have to turn elsewhere for help. Society as a whole would suffer.

Social Security actually is an excellent example of a program which provides direct and indirect benefits to many different age groups, including children. In terms of direct benefits, every working American is protected by Social Security against the risk of loss of income due to retirement, disability, or death of the family wage-earner. It is important to appreciate that social insurance, like private insurance, has a tangible worth, even if the risks that are being protected against do not materialize. For most people, this protection would have a prohibitive price tag even if it *could* be purchased from private insurers. Instead, millions of children are growing up healthy and secure today because their parents are covered under Social Security.

Because of its long-run perspective, the value of younger workers' Social Security benefits are kept up-to-date with rising wages and increases in the standard of living, assuring them that they will get back at retirement the full value of the money they put into the system throughout the course of their lives.

Young Workers

In addition, most young low-income workers can utilize the Earned Income Tax Credit to offset their Social Security contributions. Likewise, it is significant that 3,300,000 children receive survivor benefits under Social Security and that nearly 5,000,000 children under 18 reside in a home where someone receives Social Security benefits. Social Security opens employment opportunities for younger workers by encouraging older ones to retire in exchange for a pension and provides valuable survivors' benefits and payments for disabled young workers.

Perhaps most important is the economic independence that Social Security provides for older people, without which the burden of support would fall largely upon younger family members. At precisely the time that adults are struggling to rear and support their children, the responsibility for dependent parents would create enormous family stress, not to mention substantial costs.

110

The challenge of an aging society is occurring at a time of growing Federal and foreign trade deficits, cuts in domestic programs, high poverty rates among children, anxiety over economic change, and concerns about how these changes will affect the quantity and quality of opportunities available to all Americans—especially younger generations. Clearly, these often conflicting factors must be reconciled.

However, the approach adopted by so-called intergenerational "reformers" ignores the philosophy that generally is accepted by our society—one of intergenerational interdependence and support. It serves not to answer, but merely to deflect attention from the real questions, such as whether taxes need to be raised, whether growing defense expenditures are crowding out social expenditures, and whether we ought to develop new policies to meet the needs of our most vulnerable citizens, regardless of age.

The Role of Government

Likewise, the concept contributes to divisive competition between those interested in advocating policies directed primarily at particular age groups or at meeting specific needs. Such competition only will serve the interest of those wishing to reduce the role of government in providing social welfare in response to needs throughout life.

Ultimately, the misconceptions of "generational equity" could undermine critical income, health, and social service programs. Ironically, should this occur, in all probability it would be today's middle-aged and young people who would be most harmed—first because these protections would not be available when they reached old age; second, because they would have to respond individually to many of the needs of elderly relatives.

Instead of trying to destroy the very social insurance programs that have rescued millions of elderly from poverty and hunger, we ought to be expanding them to include other age groups—especially the young. With 37,000,000 Americans below the age of 65 having no health insurance at all, no other issue joins the interest of the old and the young quite as clearly.

The Interdependence of Generations

As Eric Kingson commented, "An approach to public policy that does not build on the understanding of the interdependence of all generations—or even worse, that threatens to strain the bonds between the generations—does not present a realistic framework from which to prepare for the future."

"Coddling is not how the elderly are meant or should expect to live."

Society Should Do Less for the Elderly

Henry Fairlie

In the following viewpoint, author Henry Fairlie argues that senior citizens' lobbies have convinced many people that the elderly are entitled to health care, relaxation, and wealth. He contends that simply being old should not entitle one to special treatment. Instead, government programs should help those who are in need and, according to Fairlie, far more young people are in need than old people. Fairlie is a contributing editor to *The New Republic,* a weekly journal of opinion.

As you read, consider the following questions:

1. According to the author, why do the elderly receive such a large portion of the federal budget?
2. What should be the elderly's role in society, according to Fairlie?
3. How should society change its attitudes toward the elderly, in Fairlie's opinion?

Henry Fairlie, "'Talkin' 'Bout My Generation," March 28, 1988. Reprinted by permission of THE NEW REPUBLIC, © 1988, The New Republic, Inc.

Thirty percent of the annual federal budget now goes to expenditures on people over the age of 65. Forty years from now, if the present array of programs and benefits is maintained, almost two-thirds of the budget will go to supporting and cosseting the old. Something is wrong with a society that is willing to drain itself to foster such an unproductive section of its population, one that does not even promise (as children do) one day to be productive.

Programs for the Aging

It is always difficult to question the programs for the aging because of an understandable if increasingly misdirected sympathy for them. In addition to the widespread feeling that they have earned their reward here on earth (and need not wait until they get to heaven, as the old used to expect), there is our contemporary guilt about them—and our fear. Americans still do not accept aging, dying, and death from old age itself as part of living. Of course there are the needy, the infirm, the helpless, for whom society should care. But when the old people's lobbies rally their considerable resources for a ferocious fight to protect Medicare, or to oppose a cut in the cost-of-living adjustments (COLAs) to Social Security, they are not speaking only for the needy. They are arguing for the perpetuation of a massive entitlements system for anyone and everyone over 65.

Glance through the advertisements in *Modern Maturity*, the fat, glossy magazine published by the American Association of Retired Persons—one of America's most powerful lobbies. You can be tempted by the Florida country clubs: "RETIRE IN STYLE TO FORT MYERS, FLORIDA!! . . . the New Pine Lakes Country Club. Imagine . . . acres of lakes, 18-hole golf course, tennis, heated pool, a lakeside jacuzzi, 24-hour manned security, and an unbelievable clubhouse!" Not far away the Del Tura Country Club "features Florida's finest ($3.5 million) executive golf course and clubhouse complex." Or you can buy your own ranch on the Forbes Wagon Creek Ranch in the Sangre de Cristo mountains. If all this palls, you can take a Holland America Line Alaska Cruise, with "gourmet meals, sparkling entertainment, first-class service, swimming pools, tennis courts, casinos, and million-dollar art collections." But turn the pages, and perhaps most remarkable of all, the AARP's own Travel Service offers cruises or tours to Alaska, "North to the Future." From all of this, go back to the sheaf of question-and-answer sheets setting out the AARP's arguments for almost every proposed government expenditure on the old. Something jars.

The old people's lobbying groups have proliferated in recent years. The Leadership Council of Aging Organizations (surely they do not mean "aging organizations"; if they do, one could suggest some candidates) lists 29 such groups, starting, alphabetically, with the American Association for International Aging. They range from Catholic Golden Age to the scholarly sounding Gerontology Society of America, to the once slightly notorious Gray Panthers (senior citizen urban guerrillas), to the National Association of State Units on Aging, to the United Auto Workers/Retired Members. Anyone who knows the first thing about office rentals in Washington must be impressed by the addresses of some of these groups—not least on K Street, the capital's upscale strip for the suites of the powerful industrial and commercial lobbyists.

A Special Interest Group

These groups are strong because no one, especially in election years—and it is always election year in America—dares to say a word that might offend the supposedly meek, ailing, frail, and deserving gray heads. The old have been set beside motherhood and apple pie. Yet meekness is hardly an attribute of the old in their new incarnation. And in some cases they don't even need one of the established lobbying groups to press their case before a credulous public. The notch babies, whom Timothy Noah rightly described as "spiteful, single-minded, and, to the uninitiated, deeply baffling—a parody of a special interest group," reveal the lengths to which some of the elderly now feel entitled to go in claiming benefits that aren't rightly theirs. The notch babies are the unpleasantly angry bunch of people born between 1917 and 1921 who have convinced themselves that they are being cheated out of their rightful COLA benefits.

The Rate of Poverty

Since 1970, median incomes for families headed by people 65 and over have risen more than 50 percent, after adjusting for inflation and family size, reports the Congressional Budget Office. The elderly's poverty rate is lower than the non-elderly's. The defining standard of need is poverty, not age. Once you accept that, some policies become crazy.

Robert J. Samuelson, *Newsweek*, March 21, 1988.

In fact, the AARP and most of the other groups have criticized the notch babies' claims. All the same, it is the general propaganda on behalf of the old, much of it "fired by greed, not fairness," as the *New York Times* said of the notch babies, that nurtures the clamoring and hysteria. It took only one letter to Dear Abby in 1983, and her endorsement of it (which she later partially retracted), to raise a storm on behalf of the notch babies that swept some members of Congress off their feet. . . .

Not surprisingly, over the past 30 years the elderly's standard of living has improved faster than that of younger people. Quite part from the significant increase in Social Security benefits and their protection from erosion by inflation, the Supplemental Security Income in effect guarantees them a minimum income; national health insurance is provided through Medicare; and special tax privileges protect their assets in retirement. They even receive discounts on movie and bus tickets, and much more. All of these entitlements are available to the elderly regardless of need. And while claiming that their own benefits are beyond challenge, locally the old organize to oppose tax hikes to pay for school bonds and other desirable social policies.

The history of the Older Americans Act is instructive. This simple bill authorizing funds to state agencies for a few supportive and nutritional services was passed on the heels of Medicare in 1965. When Congress extended it for another four years in 1987 (a preface to the election), the services were generously expanded. The bill is still primarily addressed to the needy old, but within it are explicit assumptions that show how its provisions can be expanded. Take the definition of "elder abuse." When we hear of "child abuse," we think specifically of certain intolerable offenses: beatings and sexual molestations. However, in many state laws the definition of "elder abuse" is so wide as to include forms of neglect that may not be neglect at all—merely leaving the old to do for themselves what they wish to do, however slowly. This is only "abuse" in the eyes of the social workers and old people's organizations, who must justify their activities and funding.

Personal Reflections

My own age gives me some standing in this matter. As I approach the arbitrary line of 65, which of course I do not consider aged, my first savoring of growing old seems to promise a time of great richness, contemplation, and absorbing interest. One not only has the years ahead, but begins to recapture the whole of one's life, in ways for which even one's middle years are unequipped. But most obviously it is less costly; one simply does not need so much. One's children are grown up and earning; one's grandchildren provide pleasure without much responsibility; mortgages are often paid off; and one need scarcely add to one's wardrobe. One is more content with simple fare in everything. It is less urgent to look for friends; one already has them, and new ones, often the young, keep turning up. In growing old, one has a stocked attic in which to rummage, and the still passing show and pageant of human life to observe, not only at a more leisurely pace, but with the convincing satisfaction and interest of having lived through many of the changes, even from their beginnings, that have brought us from there to here.

The elderly among whom I was raised did not withdraw. They may have retired from their jobs, but then they usually stayed where they were, assuming the responsibilities of a grandparent, and advising and encouraging the other young people they knew in the neighborhood. They also naturally assumed, not least in the working class and mainstream middle class, positions of leadership in the organizations, including the churches, that hold society together, so taking some of the pressure off the middle-aged and producers. They brought to them the wisdom of experience, and an unruffled, almost bustling, way of dealing with a crisis or emergency, because they had been through so many before. If I look back amazed at the time my elders found for me, then I also realize that they were not altogether selfless. I brought them news, kept them in touch, just as they brought me the otherwise inaccessible news from the immediate past. If this two-way transmission ceases, both the young and the elderly suffer.

The Aging Population

We need to penalize politicians and groups who plead for "our senior citizens" as if no distinction existed between the rich and the poor, the present or the future elderly.

The aging of the population need not force the American dream to end in this century. But it does require that we invest far more of our available resources in educating the young and more generally in raising the productivity of the next generation of workers. And it requires that we be far more prudent in the claims we make against the young, whether in the form of budget deficits, unfunded pension and health care promises, deferred maintenance of public infrastructure, or delayed cleanup of toxic wastes.

Phillip Longman, *Born to Pay*, 1987.

But suppose the old, encouraged by federal programs, siphon themselves off to places where they congregate only with other aging people. A few years ago, when I traveled around the country for five months with a companion almost a third of my age as my driver, I bought a 338-page book called *Sunbelt Retirement: The Complete State Guide to Retiring in the South and West of the United States*. Partly guided by it, I went to see some of the retirement communities, resorts, call them what one wishes. Some of them, of course, are for the rich. La Jolla, just north of San Diego, had a population of 30,000 when I was there; it also had 400 doctors. One doctor for every 75 people who anyhow are about to be called to Abraham's bosom—cite that ratio in any inner city or small town in rural America, or even in the suburbs, where the middle-aged are terrified of the possible cost of medical care for their families. And how many of those doctors catering to the old are psychiatrists, therapists, and cosmeticians? (When I was in the hospital not long ago, the nurses told me that the medical care for many elderly patients was really cosmetic, to disguise the natural process of aging.) If one needs a psychiatrist by the time one is 65, one should take the quick way out—make a swallow dive from a high bridge to the tarmac, and go to meet the Great Therapist in the Sky.

Yet it is not the rich communities that are most alarming. The vast industry of "Sunbelt Retirement" is not built on the rich. It is built on federal programs for the elderly. (And of course even those doctors in La Jolla are sustained largely by Medicare.) Most of the communities composed solely of the old are for the retired mainstream Middle Americans from the Northeast and Midwest. These are not people who have accumulated exorbitant personal assets. As soon as I reached Arizona, I realized that the Southwest is living off, and ripping off, the very "government in Washington" that it always criticizes for taxing people too much for giveaway programs to the undeserving. Huge federal subsidies to the retirement industry have replaced the military establishments, defense industries, water subsidies, and the rest that have hitherto sustained the West.

Coddling the Elderly

All the way from the Pacific to the Atlantic you can see the old lined up in banks, feeding into their accounts the checks from a range of federal agencies. The pensions and other benefits from the Veterans Administration alone are not only generous but cumulatively indefensible, since the average age of today's 27 million living veterans is 62. Every month government benefits to 91 percent of those over the age of 65 total $13.6 billion; the $50 billion per year spent on medical care for the old when Reagan took office is expected to be four times as large in the year 2000. Senator Daniel Patrick Moynihan has dryly observed that the United States may be "the first society in history in which a person is more likely to be poor if young rather than old." Moynihan's point applies even to children, 20 percent of whom live in poverty, compared with 14 percent of the elderly. It is not something to be proud of. This coddling is not how the elderly are meant or should expect to live.

The pampered ones, increasingly numerous, are rather pathetic to observe, some riding around in golf carts even on the streets, instead of taking an invigorating walk—what used to be called a "constitutional." These are not the infirm, only the naturally aging. There are no young where they live, no children, no bawling infants, no working, productive men or women. These communities frequently advertise the fact that they are "adults-only." They live with reflections of themselves. They are set apart, no longer of a piece with any larger society, with no obligations. Everything is provided. For the first time in their lives, in effect, they have servants. In vast Sun City outside Phoenix, which you reach by driving through the barrios, the legal and illegal Mexican immigrants attend to the needs of these white elders. Although they are tanned and imagine they are active, following their balls on the championship course in their carts, they in fact move as if in a mindless soft-shoe shuffle.

Millions of Old People

Of course there are millions of old people who do not live like this. Although the median income for people over 65 is now $22,000—a high figure for those who have few large purchases to make—there are still the third of the elderly blacks who live on less than $5,300. *That* is need. But the prominence of the resorts draws attention to the changed expectations of old age, among the elderly themselves, ourselves, and the society as a whole. And as in other areas, when such new expectations get lodged they take root, burgeon, and are hard to uproot, especially if they are stimulated and supported by programs that develop their own entrenched life. For it is a question not only of government, but as the gerontologist Carroll Estes has said, of ''the aging establishment . . . the congeries of programs, organizations, bureaucracies, . . . providers, industries, and professionals that serve the old in one capacity or another.'' Even if an organization like the National Council of Senior Citizens concentrates on assisting the needy and helpless, it is trapped into supporting the fat in the entitlement programs that goes to those who are not the deserving poor.

The mischief must be halted and reversed, and not least in the interest of the elderly. For one thing, there is likely to be a revolt of the working members of society when the huge baby-boom generation reaches retirement age. And as the population comes to include ever-growing numbers of young Mexicans, Central Americans, South Americans, and Asians, they too are likely to rebel, especially since their own (nuclear *and* extended) families assume so many of the traditional responsibilities of caring for the old, even in their new environment. Why should they work to indulge the white elders so generously? The old might heed another of Moynihan's predictions: that quite early in the new century the American people will be markedly brown, Spanish-speaking, young, and Catholic.

Old age must be redefined, with the majority of benefits going only to the needy. We probably will have to make stern decisions. With the increasing number of people living beyond 85, we may even have to decide that today's costly medical technologies, such as transplants, should not be provided to truly elderly people. Early retirement, especially to a self-centered and soft existence, must be discouraged. Perhaps above all, we must shake off the peculiar notion, of only recent growth, that old age is a time in which people are entitled to be rewarded for no more than performing the accepted tasks of life, or fighting in the Second World War, as many of today's elderly bleat; that if they raise a family and contribute to society by working, then when they cease to be productive they have a right to live off the still-producing like the grasshopper in the fable; that because their needs diminish, their expectations are entitled to rise.

Old People's Organizations

The old people's organizations sometimes work along these lines, as in resisting mandatory early retirement. Some have started and encouraged programs to stimulate the elderly to become productive again and remain an organic part of their society, such as working in schools as volunteers, or in special programs out of school; and of course old people are precisely those who should be well equipped to counter the basic illiteracy of even affluent children in the suburbs, the ignorance of any cultural heritage, and the decay of manners. But these efforts are marginal and sporadic, and are as nothing to the energy the lobby musters to protect the benefits for an entire class.

Meanwhile, by failing to define old age in a more limited way, by discouraging the elderly from remaining in their society, we are building a system of care that has one critical flaw. The sweeping claim of entitlements is the bubble in the whole glass house of federal assistance to the old that will eventually shatter it.

Recognizing Stereotypes

A stereotype is an oversimplified or exaggerated description of people or things. Stereotyping can be favorable. However, most stereotyping tends to be highly uncomplimentary and, at times, degrading.

Stereotyping grows out of our prejudices. When we stereotype someone, we are prejudging him or her. Consider the following example:

Whenever Mr. Johnson encounters an elderly person he automatically assumes they are slow-witted, slow-moving, forgetful, and ill-tempered; and he treats them accordingly. He has prejudged all elderly people, and it never occurs to him than an elderly person can be clear-thinking and intelligent, able-bodied, and possess a pleasant disposition.

The following statements relate to the subject matter in this chapter. Consider each statement carefully. *Mark S for any statement that is an example of stereotyping. Mark N for any statement that is not an example of stereotyping. Mark U if you are undecided about any statement.*

If you are doing this activity as a member of a class or group, compare your answers with those of other class or group members. Be able to defend your answers. You may discover that others will come to different conclusions than you do. Listening to the reasons others present their answers may give you valuable insights in recognizing stereotypes.

S = *stereotype*
N = *not a stereotype*
U = *undecided*

1. Old people are helpless.

2. More of the elderly are economically secure than they were a generation ago.

3. Most old people have hoarded their money and now they want the government to give them all sorts of financial help too.

4. All old people expect far too much from society. They want the government to pay all of their expenses and they don't want anyone to complain.

5. Older and younger generations can get along well and contribute to each others' lives.

6. The government discriminates against the elderly by basing the poverty line on age.

7. Many older people, especially older women, are living well below the poverty line.

8. I just love old women. They're all so sweet and grandmotherly.

9. The elderly deserve to have help paying for health care and to have pensions and Social Security. They worked hard all their lives, after retirement they deserve to relax and not worry about money.

10. Retirement can be a time of personal growth and fulfillment.

11. Old people have nothing to worry about. They have no responsibilities for work or family. They can spend all their time going to the beach, playing golf, and spending their money. Old age is a wonderful time of life.

12. Old people have no money and no way of getting more. Old age is terrible.

13. The elderly are often ignored by our youth-oriented culture.

14. The older members of families are just a burden on the younger ones.

15. Government assistance for the elderly has not prevented poverty.

16. The old and the young are not competing for government money. Programs for the elderly benefit younger generations and vice versa.

Periodical Bibliography

The following articles have been selected to supplement the diverse views presented in this chapter.

Melinda Beck	"The Geezer Boom," *Newsweek*, special issue, Winter/Spring 1990.
Gary Stanley Becker	"Social Security Should Benefit Only the Elderly Poor," *Business Week*, January 16, 1989.
Horace B. Deets	"We Must End Age Discrimination," *Modern Maturity*, December 1988/January 1989.
Richard Easterlin	"The Economy: Old Get Richer While Young Get Poorer," *USA Today*, July/August 1988.
Robert England	"Aging in America: Wealth and the Elderly," *Current*, July/August 1987.
Fortune	"The Senior Boom: How It Will Change America," March 27, 1989.
Dorcas R. Hardy	"Social Security's Insecure Future," *The Wall Street Journal*, August 21, 1989.
Patricia Horn	"Elders on the Edge," *Dollars & Sense*, January/February 1988.
Michael D. Hurd	"The Economic Status of the Elderly," *Science*, May 12, 1989.
John E. Jacob	"Ageism," *Vital Speeches of the Day*, March 15, 1988.
Anne McGrath	"Twilight Self-Sufficiency," *U.S. News & World Report*, August 3, 1987.
Linda Marsa	"Securing the Golden Years," *Black Enterprise*, December 1988.
Modern Maturity	"Taking the Fear Out of Finances," December 1988/January 1989.
Robert J. Samuelson	"The Elderly Aren't Needy," *Newsweek*, March 21, 1988.
Maurice Weinrobe	"Liberating Home Equity of the Elderly Benefits All," *The Wall Street Journal*, December 8, 1988.

CHAPTER

3

Is Social Security Necessary for the Elderly?

Chapter Preface

President Franklin Roosevelt introduced Social Security in 1935 to help guarantee each working person a minimum retirement income. Theoretically, what people pay into Social Security while they are working will be paid back to them after retirement. However, the aging of the largest segment of the population, the post-World War II baby boom generation, causes many to fear Social Security will collapse. Critics such as *Fortune* magazine contributor Lee Smith argue that the baby boom retirees will rapidly use up Social Security's cash reserves and bankrupt the system. According to Smith, Social Security should be reformed before the baby boomers retire.

Supporters of Social Security, however, contend that it is a successful system. Authors Joan and Merton Bernstein argue that Social Security not only will remain solvent into the twenty-first century but also, for a time, will show a $12 trillion surplus. The baby boomers, the Bernsteins conclude, will not overtax the system.

The authors in the following chapter debate the present and future success of the Social Security program.

"Few myths have the currency and credence of the notion that the elderly are affluent, or at least better off than their juniors."

Social Security Is Fair

Merton C. Bernstein and Joan Brodshaug Bernstein

In the following viewpoint, Merton C. Bernstein and Joan Brodshaug Bernstein object to the perception that Social Security helps wealthy senior citizens at the expense of impoverished young people. According to the Bernsteins, without Social Security many of the elderly would be living in poverty. They contend that senior citizens are entitled to the benefits they receive. Merton C. Bernstein is the Coles Professor of Law at Washington University in St. Louis, Missouri, and co-author with his wife, Joan, of the book, *Social Security: The System That Works.* Joan Brodshaug Bernstein has been the administrator of several non-profit agencies.

As you read, consider the following questions:

1. Why do the authors believe that even with fewer workers paying in to Social Security, the system will remain solvent?
2. How do the authors portray the financial situation of the elderly? How does Social Security affect the elderly's finances?
3. Why do the Bernsteins argue that Social Security is successful?

Merton C. Bernstein and Joan Brodshaug Bernstein, "Politics and the Elderly: Toward a Sharing of Resources," May 9, 1988. Reprinted by permission from FORTUNE Magazine; © 1988 Time Inc. All rights reserved.

A nationally syndicated editorial cartoon recently showed a corpulent, cane-carrying, white-haired lady brandishing a sub-machine gun. The caption read: "The reason Congress doesn't touch Social Security . . . Granbo." The cartoon's message: Elder power keeps Congress from doing what it should—cutting Social Security, especially its cost-of-living adjustments (COLAs). Many businessmen, economists, editorial writers, and even a few politicians express the hope that the National Economic Commission will enable the President to do the unthinkable—shrink Social Security benefits to reduce the budget deficit.

A $50 Billion Surplus

But Social Security does not cause federal deficits. Indeed, over its first 50 years Social Security operated at a more than $50 billion (yes, billion) *surplus*, and during the period 1987-92 it will produce a $330 billion reserve, with a multitrillion (yes, trillion) dollar surplus in prospect for the early decades of the next century. Why the clamor for cuts, caps, delays, or other reductions in COLAs? Because Social Security is a great cash cow: It pays so many beneficiaries, some 38 million, that seemingly small benefit reductions would produce even larger surpluses.

Since Social Security is funded through payroll taxes, shared equally by employer and employee, the government kept the account separate from the rest of the budget for the first 32 years. Then, in 1969, President Johnson began including Social Security accounts in the general budget, hoping thereby to screen the deficits caused by the Vietnam war. In 1983, in response to a recommendation by the national Commission on Social Security Reform, Congress restored Social Security's separateness. Supposedly. But the Gramm-Rudman-Hollings deficit reduction law requires Social Security receipts and payout to be calculated with the rest of budgeted government revenues and spending. . . .

Social Security *seemingly* offers the only possible source of deficit relief. But it would be a mistake to cut COLAs or subject Social Security recipients to means testing.

That's not to say that all old-age benefits are sacrosanct. Some can certainly be spared to help the cause of deficit reduction. For example: Taxing Social Security benefits more extensively makes sound tax policy because it would treat all income alike and would affect mainly upper-income recipients. In addition, Congress could pare down some of the tax breaks in employee retirement programs, such as stock-bonus, profit-sharing, and 401(k) plans. Such plans enable employees, largely the best paid, to shield earnings from tax until drawn as benefits. The Congressional Budget Office calls these tax-favored retirement plans "one of the largest preferences in the federal income tax" to survive tax reform.

Before the 1986 tax cut, eventual taxation of benefits would have recaptured most of the lost revenues. But the rate cuts sliced about $13.6 billion a year from those deferred collections. Congress ought to recapture that annual $13.6 billion by taxing benefits at 1986 rates for contributions made prior to that time. This would result in collecting what people expected to pay and what Congress expected the Treasury to receive.

Lost Earnings

That brings us back to Granbo. The caricature depicts her with symbols of affluence, including what appears to be a fur coat. Shades of yesterday's fiction of mink-coated welfare cheats! But Social Security is not welfare; it is a substitute for earnings lost through retirement. Social Security eligibility comes from working long enough in "covered" jobs and contributing payroll taxes.

Few myths have the currency and credence of the notion that the elderly are affluent, or at least better off than their juniors. But according to a 1987 Social Security Administration study, about 80% of Social Security beneficiaries had no earnings. For that group, the median total income was $8,410; of that, $6,270 came from Social Security benefits. About one-fifth of all beneficiaries had income over $20,000; of that, only one-fifth came from Social Security, much of it subject to income tax. Work income (often earned by an as yet unretired spouse) put many into the over-$20,000 category—temporarily. For most people, however, job opportunities diminish after age 62, and relatively few work past 65.

A Family Program

Most people think that only old age retirement is covered by Social Security. This is a serious misunderstanding. Social Security also pays monthly life insurance benefits to persons in midlife (between 20 and 65) and to their families. In addition, it pays Medicare hospital insurance benefits not only to the aged but to younger people who have serious disabilities.

Social Security benefits may be paid over an individual's entire lifespan from birth to death. It is not simply an old age program. It is a family program.

Wilbur J. Cohen, "Social Security Is Here to Stay," August 1988.

So why does the myth of affluence continue? One reason is that some analyses of the economic status of those 65 and over include a wealthy fraction, some of whom are still in the work force and do not even draw Social Security benefits because of high earnings from their jobs. When their income is figured into the 65-and-over group, atypically high *average* (mean) income results. For instance, if one person in a group of ten gets an annual income of

$100,000 and each of the other nine gets $10,000, their average (mean) income is $19,000. In contrast, their median income (half with an income above and half below) is $10,000, a more accurate portrayal of the financial situation of most members of the group.

Spendable Income

In 1985 the Council of Economic Advisers fueled the myth by reporting that among families headed by a person 65 or over, 1983 mean income was an impressive $21,420, and the mean for individuals was a solid $10,040. However, 60.8% of those individuals had pretax income of only $4,000 to $15,000. A report by the Conference Board and the Census Bureau the same year furthered the misconception, stating that the elderly had more "spendable discretionary income" than any other age group. The study defined discretionary income as that amount 30% or more above the average income for the age group. The income of many over-65s qualified as discretionary because the group's average income was so low. Only those under 25 had lower dollar income—just what everyone would expect of young people, many of them at school, unemployed, or on the bottom rungs of the work force.

Much has also been made of the fact that during the 1970s those 65 and over enjoyed a bigger advance in average income than the "nonaged," with Social Security benefits accounting for most of the increase. But from 1947 to 1967, the income of the elderly lagged woefully, with shockingly high numbers in poverty. That led Congress to improve the Social Security payouts. By the early 1980s, the elderly drew about even with the nonelderly.

Some critics contend that the elderly are well off because of their assets, especially homes, their larger federal income tax exemptions and state property tax breaks, and the fact that they no longer have expenses associated with employment. A high percentage of those 65 and older *do* own their own homes, often mortgage-free. But older homes are a mixed blessing, frequently needing more repair and maintenance than recently built boxes. Besides, property taxes often are high, and most state and local tax breaks go to only a fraction of the elderly who demonstrate very low income. In 1986 Congress eliminated the extra deduction for the elderly. And anyone who thinks that not going to work saves money hasn't paid oil and gas bills for full days spent at home.

Comparisons of aged/nonaged often do not take into account the many tax advantages enjoyed by the *non*aged, such as deductible mortgage interest, untaxed employer health insurance contributions, and the breaks given deferred income. In fact, most elderly Americans have modest incomes and depend heavily on modest Social Security benefits. For them cutting, capping, or freezing COLAs would mean a loss of badly needed purchasing power. . . .

That leaves the argument suggested by former Commerce Secretary Peter G. Peterson and others that Social Security should be "means tested," that is, restricted only to those who demonstrate by their low income and meager assets that they are needy. In 1983, David Stockman, who was then the Budget Director, testified that without Social Security, the incomes of over half the elderly (55.1%) would have dropped below the poverty level; with it, the figure was still 14.6%.

Social Security Benefits

Each month more than 38 million Americans receive Social Security benefits—having earned them either directly (because of contributions made during their working lives) or indirectly (because of contributions made by working family members). Benefits go to:

3 million disabled workers and their spouses
3 million children of deceased or disabled workers
5 million widows
27 million retirees and their spouses

In addition, more than 130 million American workers who are contributing to the system through earnings deductions are building the earned right to future retirement benefits for themselves and their dependents; disability benefits to protect them and their dependents in the event of severe, long-term disability; and, when they die, survivor benefits for their spouses and dependent children or parents.

Save Our Security, "Social Security: Crucial Questions & Straight Answers," January 1989.

Means testing would force millions of formerly self-supporting and self-respecting people to suffer the indignity of proving their destitution. Many—especially older people who have always earned their own way—already forgo benefits like food stamps because they will not submit to such procedures. Furthermore, needs testing may discourage many from saving if reserves of cash and property disqualify them from benefits. Not least, needs-testing programs tend to be expensive: The Social Security cash programs cost just over 1% of payout to operate, while Supplemental Security Income (SSI), the comparable means-tested program for the very poor, costs 9%.

Most Americans support Social Security because it preserves a modicum of human dignity and independence for our parents, the disabled, 3.2 million children with disabled, retired, or deceased parents, and, sooner or later, ourselves. The trustees of the Social Security funds say the program can meet its obligations over the next 75 years. Everyone can rely on it. For how many things in this world can that be said?

"Reordering priorities would only begin with Social Security. For us, the aged, the question is: Do we care enough to share?"

Social Security Is Unfair

Harold E. Fey

The author of the following viewpoint, Harold E. Fey, contends that the elderly receive more than their share of funds through Social Security. By offering Social Security benefits to the elderly, Fey argues, the government is unable to fund programs that would benefit poor children, the unemployed, and working parents. Thus Fey writes, Social Security unfairly denies help to those who need it—younger people. Fey is a retired editor of *The Christian Century*, a weekly Christian magazine.

As you read, consider the following questions:

1. Why does Fey write that the elderly discriminate against younger generations?
2. How should Social Security be changed, according to the author?
3. What is the relationship between Social Security and education, according to Fey?

Harold E. Fey, "Politics and the Elderly: Toward a Sharing of Resources." Copyright 1988 Christian Century Foundation. Reprinted by permission from the December 14, 1988 issue of *The Christian Century*.

Inequities in the distribution of what have come to be called "entitlements" need to receive more attention in American society. The disproportion of public funds paid to the elderly as over against payments and services to children is a scandal, but almost nobody is scandalized. A look at the facts and a little speculation concerning the consequences of the disparity are in order.

A Large Disparity

In the discussion that follows, my indebtedness to Phillip Longman's *Born to Pay: The New Politics of Aging in America* is substantial. Longman identifies the key fact by quoting a 1977 study by economists Spencer Spengler and Robert Clark: "Expenditures for the elderly at all levels of government exceed the amount spent on children, age seventeen and under, including the total amount spent on public education, by more than three to one." Noting that "the disparity is much larger today," Longman states that "Social Security pensions and Medicare pensions have become much more generous while welfare and educational programs for the young have been cut." He adds: "At the federal level, the disproportion is about ten to one.". . .

Our nation is suffering and will suffer more from our comparative neglect of our children. Neither the public nor the government takes seriously the findings of several national commissions which have deplored this neglect of the younger generation.

Reasons for the disparate treatment of the old and the young include the simple fact that elders vote and children do not. Entitlements for the elderly have become the sacred cow of American politics. Officeholders and candidates threaten entitlements at their peril. One of the most powerful lobbies in Washington is run by the 29-million member American Association of Retired Persons—which *Newsweek* recently described as "the big gray money machine.". . .

Another reason for the disproportionate public expenditure on the elderly is the population's greater longevity. Says Longman: "In 1900 only four percent of Americans had managed to reach the age of sixty-five or older. . . . In recent years life expectancy among the elderly has been increasing faster than any other age group." A recent pension fund bulletin states that "in 1950 among those who reached sixty-five and older only one in eight could expect to reach their ninetieth birthday. Today one in four Americans who have reached the age of sixty-five will live to see their ninetieth birthday. In fact, the group of Americans eighty and over is growing five times faster than the rest of the population. . . . In about two decades this segment of the population will double in size."

A hundred years ago when Chancellor Bismarck in Germany established the first social security system, he set the retirement age at 65 because only a small minority reached that age. When President Franklin Roosevelt created the U.S. Social Security System in 1935, the median life expectancy was 63.7 years. So it was not expected that the number of people claiming pensions would be large. But now the over-65 contingent is 12 percent of the population and is growing rapidly. The pressure on legislators to keep up the so-called entitlements has become a powerful political force.

Serious Concerns

Young as well as old have serious concerns about the future solvency and relevancy of Social Security and Medicare.

In a healthy, long-lived culture, many people will question the appropriateness of generous government support based on age, when there are so many people of all ages who are desperately needy.

And there is most definitely a growing discomfort among the young with the quickly rising power of the elderly.

Ken Dychtwald, *Age Wave*, 1989.

The skewing of our national financial priorities lies in the peculiar nature of the Social Security System. As of now, workers are taxed 7.15 percent of their salaries, and their employers pay an equal amount. The total of the two halves of this tax is soon to reach 15 percent. The income from it is divided into three funds: 70 percent goes to the Old Age and Survivors Insurance Fund, 20 percent into Medicare and Hospital Assistance and 10 percent into a fund for disabled workers of any age. In 1983 the expenditure on senior citizens over 65 was $217 billion, or about $7,700 per claimant. Wages under $2,000 are not subject to taxes. (People earning over $45,000 are taxed 7.5 percent of their income.) In 1983 monthly checks went out to 34.2 million persons.

What happens to the money collected each year on the payroll tax? According to Philip Rowland, under current law the Social Security Administration must spend the entire sum within the year it is collected. First, the millions of claimants receive their entitlements. All money in excess of their claims must be turned over to the U.S Treasury. Says Rowland: "The Treasury in turn uses the funds either to reduce the government's current deficits or to finance the government debt." To recompense the Social Security Administration, the Treasury issues long-term government bonds in the amount it borrows. These bonds, which draw interest, are being held by the Social Security Administration until they come due in the 21st century. At that time, where will the government find money to redeem its bonds, which in effect are promissory notes? It must be provided by the taxpayers of that distant day—by the children of the babyboomers. So the discrimination in entitlements now imposed on the young will be imposed on them in another form when they become taxpayers.

Lending Social Security Money

"Any funds Social Security lends to the Treasury are supposed to be returned with interest," Rowland points out. Even at a low rate of interest, the obligation will double when it accumulates over many years. According to Rowland, it is future taxpayers who will be liable for the IOU's, "come what may." If Social Security does not receive back the money it lends, along with the agreed interest, the Old Age, Medicare and disability funds will go broke that much sooner. An article in the September 29, 1988 issue of the *Los Angeles Times* predicts that "although tax revenue from workers will continue to exceed payments to retirees until 2030, that will change radically as the baby-boom hordes begin to reach retirement age." The article also notes that the Social Security Administration will collect $262 billion in taxes in 1988 from workers and their employers. It will spend $222 billion for entitlements; "the remaining $40 billion will go into a special bond issue legally isolated from other government programs."

American society has enough problems without adding a struggle between generations, but such a struggle will come unless we recognize and deal with what is happening. Whereas 3.2 persons' payroll taxes now support each elderly pensioner, the decline in the birthrate ensures that for every pensioner only three or perhaps two persons will be paying into Social Security in the years when today's workers arrive at the age to collect their pensions. While the wage level may continue to rise, that is not at all certain.

Wages depend in the last analysis upon productivity, and productivity depends upon the education and training of the producer. Educational standards in the U.S. have been falling. Many high school graduates cannot read or write at the level needed in an economy dominated by high technology. A situation in which fewer and more poorly educated wage earners are called upon to support a larger number of elderly nonproducers is clearly in prospect. Future taxpayers can carry the load only if they are equipped with a higher level of education. And if we are to have more sophisticated workers, a larger proportion of the nation's resources must be devoted to improving education.

It also means that the moral question involved in the present inequity must be faced. It is simply not right for today's elderly to appropriate for themselves resources and prerogatives in a way that discriminates against their own children and grandchildren. It is not right for the young to be born into a situation in which they will be taxed to support their elders at a higher standard of living than they can possibly have when they reach retirement age.

The importance of equal treatment of the young has been raised by several educational and financial groups. In 1981 the National Commission on Excellence in Education was appointed by Secretary of Education T.H. Bell. Eighteen eminent persons studied the problem and reported in 1985 that "our nation is at risk." The commission did not mince words:

> Our once unchallenged pre-eminence in commerce, industry, science and technical innovation is being overtaken by competitors throughout the world. . . . The educational foundations of our society are presently being eroded by a rising tide of mediocrity that threatens our very future as a nation and a people. What was unimaginable a generation ago has begun to occur—others are matching and surpassing our educational attainments. . . . We have done it to ourselves—squandered the gains made after Sputnik, dismantled our educational support systems.

The tone of grave concern runs throughout the report, yet its impact on our government has been negligble. . . .

The commission's conclusion made one point of special relevance to the elderly: "The search for solutions for our educational problems must also include commitment to life-long learning." The dynamic nature of modern society requires nothing less.

Steve Benson. Reprinted by permission: Tribune Media Services.

The report notes that education must prepare the 1.5 million young people who graduate each year from some level of schooling to join their elders in continuous striving for new attainments. This applies to the ''seventy-five per cent of the work force now employed [who] will still be working in 2000 A.D. All will need further education and retraining if we as a nation are to achieve and prosper. The goal is a learning society—learning more as the world itself changes.''

Lifelong Learning

Commitment to lifelong learning does not exclude the elderly. The old dream of retirement as a period of purposeless drifting or obsessive pursuit of little white golf balls is giving way to more creative energy. After they retire, businesspeople often help younger people to start businesses or to solve problems. Ministers volunteer to serve churches or social organizations. Some lawyers serve as reconcilers or arbitrators to keep disputes out of court. Colleges and universities find many older people in classes. Women are often more successful than men in making constructive use of their time, which may help explain why they generally live longer than men. With so many women joining the work force, the wide spectrum of volunteer organizations is increasingly dependent on older citizens for service as well as support.

Sharing Resources

Commitment to lifelong learning exists, but it could be stronger among the elderly—and it will be stronger when we elderly discover and employ better ways to share our resources and power with the children of America. We know how to use political processes for our own advantage. Now we must learn how to use political power to bring equal advantages to our children's children. The Social Security Act should be amended to include provisions for child health and welfare. A cutback in Social Security's cost-of-living adjustment would save $5 to $10 billion a year, says Roger Strauss, cochair of a bipartisan commission seeking ways to reduce the national budget deficit. Stopping Social Security payments to the rich would save more. Raising the retirement age would also help. Such steps would free funds which could be used to lift the level of excellence in the education of the young, thereby restoring balance and establishing equity. Reordering priorities would only begin with Social Security. For us, the aged, the question is: Do we care enough to share?

3

VIEWPOINT

"The social security fund is solvent and will remain so for the foreseeable future."

Social Security Benefits Should Be Expanded

Dollars & Sense

In the following viewpoint, the editors of *Dollars & Sense* argue that the Social Security system has remained popular and successful throughout its existence. They contend that Social Security will continue to be available for everyone for many years in the future. *Dollars & Sense* is a monthly socialist magazine.

As you read, consider the following questions:

1. Why do the authors believe Social Security benefits everyone?
2. How do Social Security opponents undermine confidence in the system, according to the authors?
3. How do the editors of *Dollars & Sense* discount the "generational equity" argument?

Dollars & Sense, "Old and Enduring," January/February 1988. Reprinted by permission of Dollars & Sense, 1 Summer Street, Somerville, Massachusetts 02143.

For many people in this country, the words "social security" call up very mixed feelings. On the one hand, they think of basic financial security in old age, a safety net to catch those whose savings and pensions don't suffice. On the other hand, they think of media images of a funding system wracked by crisis, a well-organized senior lobby looting young workers' paychecks, and the terrifying prospect of 75 million elderly baby-boomers sucking the economy dry in the early decades of the next century. In short, social security helps a lot, but can we really afford it?

The Heart of Social Security

The social security program most definitely helps a large number of Americans. The heart of social security is its old age, survivors, and disability insurance (OASDI) program, which gives 90% of the labor force a sense of certainty about their future and lifts millions of older Americans out of poverty. Without social security benefits, the number of elder poor would roughly quadruple from 3.3 million to 12.8 million, and the percentage of those over 65 with incomes below the poverty line would jump from 12.4% to 47.6% (based on 1984 figures, the most recent available for social security).

Meanwhile, most of the negative aspects of social security's image are undeserved. Contrary to the claims of many conservative doomsayers, the social security system is not headed towards financial disaster. The social security fund is solvent and will remain so for the foreseeable future.

In fact, the problem with social security is not that it transfers too much income to the old, but that it doesn't transfer enough. The benefits are modest, replacing only 41% of the income of workers with average earnings. In the Reagan years of austerity, however, the federal government has sidelined any proposals for a more generous and equitable program. Instead, conservative politicians have cried crisis in order to push—so far unsuccessfully—for a rollback of existing benefits.

New Deal Legacy

Like many products of the New Deal, social security originated as a compromise proposal that reflected the concerns of U.S. capitalists as well as those of U.S. workers. Although President Roosevelt originally supported a program funded out of general revenues from the income tax, Republicans and southern Democrats compelled him to agree to finance social security with regressive payroll taxes which are borne almost entirely by workers. They also insisted that workers' benefits be tied to their contributions, ensuring that social security would not be used to redistribute income from the well-off to poorer workers. Social security's universal coverage has won it broad public approval. While programs such as Aid to Families with Dependent Children, which support only the poorest segment of the population, have waxed and waned in popularity, social security has enjoyed lasting popular support.

Since 1935, Congress has gradually expanded the scope of the social security program. Congress added benefits for spouses and surviving dependents of covered workers in 1939, and disability payments in 1956. In 1965 President Johnson won approval for the Medicare and Medicaid health insurance programs which are run by the Social Security Administration. Over the same period of time, Congress extended coverage from the initial set of commercial and industrial occupations to agricultural and service sector jobs. Finally, in 1983 Congress brought new federal civilian employees and the employees of nonprofit organizations into the program. Now more than 90% of the jobs in the economy are covered.

Conservatives, however, have never been happy with social security, and in the austere 1980s their criticisms have gained adherents. The conservatives challenge both the basic principles of the social security program and its fiscal viability. On the level of principle, the conservative critique claims that social security is coercive. The 124 million workers paying payroll taxes have no choice but to contribute towards their retirement.

Financial Soundness

The 1983 Social Security reforms were designed to maintain the system's financial soundness for the next 75 years with only modest tax increases. By the time the baby boomers retire, they will have built up a trust fund surplus on the order of $2 trillion that they can draw on to help lighten the burden on their children. Beyond 75 years, no one's crystal ball is good enough to support sensible debate.

Social Security is not "welfare for the middle class," as Peter G. Peterson and other critics so often maintain. It is a retirement program for everyone. And on efficiency grounds alone, it's a clear winner. It is portable, inflation-adjusted and progressive in its benefits structure (low-income workers pay taxes on a larger part of their wages but get back higher rates of return). The whole system operates with an overhead rate of only one percent.

Forrest Chisman, *The Washington Post National Weekly Edition*, December 28, 1987.

But the case for compulsory, government-provided pensions is a strong one. Compulsory retirement coverage makes sense because the community would otherwise have to support those who might voluntarily choose not to provide for their old age. In addition, government involvement is essential because the private market couldn't provide old age insurance at a fair rate. The problem is one of "adverse selection": in a private insurance market, those who expect to live a long time after retiring would be eager to purchase annuities—yearly payments of constant amounts—while those who expect short retirements would be reluctant to buy. Private insurers would thus expect the bulk of their customers to be of the first type, and hence would have to charge inflated prices in order to break even. The average customer would wind up being able to afford less insurance than he or she might desire.

Since the late 1930s, the vast majority of U.S. citizens has supported government provision of retirement insurance. Conservative presidential candidates—such as Alf Landon and Barry Goldwater—who have called for making the system "voluntary" have routinely gone down in flames. (Ronald Reagan got away with a similar proposal in 1980 primarily because no one believed he was serious.) Consensus about the principle of social security, however, has not prevented continued attacks on the program.

Can We Afford It?

Much of the conservative criticism focuses on whether the social security system can pay for itself. Before 1983, current workers were not accumulating a surplus fund from which they would later receive benefits. Instead, in what was known as the "pay-as-you-go" system, workers' payroll taxes went to provide benefits to current retirees. When one generation of workers retired, there was certain to be a new generation of employees willing and able to pay for them—just as they had paid for their predecessors.

However, when U.S. economic growth sagged in the mid-1970s, a chorus of "experts" began to argue that the social security system would collapse because future generations of workers would be unable or unwilling to pay for the retirement of the baby boom. By the early 1980s, belief in the reality of the crisis was widespread.

What caused all the concern? With a pay-as-you-go system, each generation must have enough workers paying social security taxes to cover the benefits of the current retirees. For the rest of this century, demographers estimate that there will be three or more workers paying taxes for each retiree. But around 2010 the number of workers per retiree will begin to fall precipitously, and will reach a low of about two at mid-century. Put the other way around, the number of retirees per worker is due to rise sharply, and many experts claim that the burden will be more than future workers can—or should—bear.

This argument, however, overlooks the fact that the total number of dependents per worker—counting children as well as retirees—will be lower in the 21st century than it is now. The average number of dependents per worker, which was 1.42 in

1970, is projected to fall to 1.26 in 2025, and to remain at that level through 2050. Since the costs of maintaining young and old dependents are roughly the same, the overall dependency "burden" on those working will also be lower.

Someone, though, is going to have to pay for the baby boom's golden years, and a good deal of the debate in the early 1980s concerned who that should be. By passing the 1983 social security reform bill, Congress decided that today's workers should pick up most of the tab. The new law gradually raises both payroll taxes and the age of eligibility for benefits, and taxes the social security benefits of those with higher than average incomes. As a result, the OASDI trust fund has already begun accumulating surpluses which will reach over a quarter of the gross national product in 2020, only to be drawn down to nearly zero when the baby boom retires in the 30 years that follow.

A Tremendous Contribution

Social Security has made and is making a tremendous contribution to the strengthening of the social, economic, political and moral life of our nation. Those who seek to weaken the foundation on which it rests are rendering America a great disservice. Those who seek to strengthen the foundation, however, are rendering a service not only to this generation, but to generations yet unborn.

Arthur Flemming, *The National Forum*, 1986.

If the measures passed in the reform bill stay in effect, the financial stability of the OASDI program appears to be assured—assuming, of course, that nothing prevents the continuation of modest long-term economic growth. Opposition to the final stages of the payroll tax, however, is already brewing in Congress. Since current law requires the OASDI surplus to be invested in federal bonds that finance the deficit, conservatives such as Jack Kemp are concerned that its build-up will reduce the pressure to cut domestic spending.

In spite of the uncertainty surrounding exactly how the baby boomers' retirement will be financed, there is no doubt that the economy can afford it. But critics of the whole social security concept do have one last argument in their repertoire. Michael Boskin, author of *Too Many Promises: The Uncertain Future of Social Security* (1986), typifies those who grudgingly concede that social security need not go broke, but also maintain that the system is tremendously unfair. Boskin even foresees "a confrontation between workers and retirees . . . that will create the greatest polarization along economic lines in our society since the Civil War."

According to Boskin, those who are already retired or who retire in the near future will get a much better "deal"—in terms of benefits per dollar of contributions—than those who retire after the year 2000. Boskin's argument may be formally correct, but he ignores the fact that, given even modest economic growth over the next decades, current youngsters will have higher lifetime incomes than current retirees, and thus will have greater wealth to share. Even if economic growth is slow, the burden on today's young could be lessened by funding social security from sources other than the payroll tax.

Progressive Prospects?

Since social security is neither financially unsound nor grossly unfair to the under-60 crowd, radical cuts in benefits are neither necessary nor desirable. Indeed, benefits should be expanded for groups currently covered inadequately. For instance, social security's treatment of women needs to be changed. Under current law, divorced women who were married less than ten years receive no share of the credit for their ex-husband's earnings. As a consequence, they obtain social security benefits only if they have qualified on their own. Even when they are able to do so, their benefits are often considerably lower than those they would have been entitled to if they had remained married.

Congress has refused to address the problem, although it has begun to investigate one possible remedy, that of "earnings sharing." Under the various earnings-sharing schemes, the payroll taxes contributed by a husband and wife would be credited equally to each. If the marriage should end, each of the ex-partners would keep his or her share of the credits. Many of the earnings-sharing proposals have serious problems. Since they take for granted that no additional revenues can be raised, most of the proposals involve cutting the benefits of some recipients in order to aid divorced women.

Congress could overcome the problems with the earnings-sharing proposals—and with benefit adequacy in general—if it were willing to expand the program's funding. There is no reason the burden of funding should fall exclusively on workers. The social security system could be used to redistribute income from rich to poor. By removing the $43,800 cap on wages subjected to the payroll tax, high-paid workers would share the burden more equally with low-paid workers. Better yet, the social security tax could be financed through the income tax, a progressive tax that falls on property income as well as wages.

While conservatives have not succeeded in dismantling social security, they have succeeded in distracting attention from progressive social security reform. Despite the conservative scare stories, the real barrier to a more equitable social security system is not economic constraint but political reluctance.

"To avoid a war between the generations, the support system for the elderly should be reformed now, while Social Security trust funds still are flush."

Social Security Benefits Should Be Reduced

Lee Smith

Lee Smith contributes to *Fortune* magazine. In the following viewpoint, Smith argues that the entire Social Security system is in trouble. He asserts that Social Security will begin running out of money in the first half of the next century. He contends that the system should be reformed to prevent the money shortage.

As you read, consider the following questions:

1. What are Social Security's main problems, according to the author?
2. What changes in the system does Smith advocate?
3. According to Smith, how could Social Security affect the relationship between the elderly and those not yet retired?

Lee Smith, "The War Between the Generations," *Fortune*, July 20, 1987. © 1987 Time Inc. All rights reserved. Excerpted with permission from *Reader's Digest*, June 1988.

''A pig in a python'' is what demographers call the baby boom, that troublesome lump of 75 million Americans born between 1946 and 1964. Almost one-third of today's population, the boomers have distended society at every stage of their lives, overcrowding schools in the 1950s and upending the nation's values in the '60s and '70s. The worst is yet to come.

Social Security Benefits

Boomers are likely to demand the same retirement benefits they now pay their parents through mandatory contributions to Social Security under the Federal Insurance Contributions Act (FICA). And boomers will probably want even more in Medicare benefits, because they are going to live longer. The younger, smaller generation that is supposed to pay for these goodies may refuse.

To avoid a war between the generations, the support system for the elderly should be reformed now, while Social Security trust funds still are flush. ''The assumption that each working generation will take care of the one that preceded it is finished,'' says Sen. David F. Durenberger (R., Minn.), founder of Americans for Generational Equity (AGE).

At the moment, the biggest part of Social Security is purring along smoothly. FICA contributions have so exceeded outlays for the old-age, survivors and disability insurance programs (OASDI) that these trust funds have swelled to $67 billion. As boomers move into peak earning years, the funds should increase to $1.3 trillion by the year 2000.

Another part of the program, however, is disturbing. By 2002, according to government projections, the high cost of health care will help eat up the $103-billion Medicare trust fund. To keep making hospital payments, Congress could raise payroll taxes again. But it probably will take the easy way out and shift billions from the robust OASDI funds into Medicare.

Declining Birthrates

Even without that jolt, the entire system is headed off a cliff. Since 1965, the annual number of births has been declining. Today 3.3 workers toil to support a single beneficiary. By 2010, when the first boomers near 65, only 2.9 workers will be around to do the job. The Social Security trust funds will shrink drastically after 2030, when the support ratio withers to 1.9 workers per beneficiary.

To slow this headlong plunge, the reserves must be managed wisely. As OASDI funds grow fatter, Congress will be tempted to use them not just to bail out Medicare but to expand all payments to retirees, who vote in greater numbers than other age groups. The reserves must be husbanded for the boomer's big retirement party or Social Security will go broke.

Even if Congress keeps its hands off the reserves, in the long run the boomers' demands will still throw Social Security into deficit. Initial retirement benefits are tied to wages, and real wages have been flat over the last 15 years. To give retired boomers the same percentage of their preretirement income that today's elderly receive, and similar medical care, workers of the future may have to turn over as much as 40 percent of their paychecks. It is impossible to believe they will be so generous.

Solutions that avoid forcing future wage earners to pay more are politically tempting, but seem unworkable. Phillip Longman, 32, author of *Born to Pay*, a look at the new politics of aging in America, suggests that one option might be to swell the future labor force through tax incentives for having more children. People without children, for example, could be taxed to finance day-care centers; it will be other people's children, after all, who will take care of childless retirees. But, as Longman points out, France has tried tax incentives for years with little success.

Social Security

Another tactic would be to allow more immigration. The United States could try to increase current immigration levels of about 600,000 to, say, 1.7 million. But a flood of immigrants would probably not appeal to organized labor.

Long-Term Solvency

The 75 million members of the Baby Boom generation—all those Americans born between 1946 and 1964—have good reason to fear desertion by their successors. Unless many fundamental trends are soon reversed, the Baby Boomers are headed for a disastrous retirement.

The long-term solvency of the Social Security system has come to depend on several broad contingencies, none of which seems very likely in the lifetime of the Baby Boom generation.

Phillip Longman, *The Atlantic Monthly*, June 1985.

Since the supply of Social Security contributors is not likely to rise, the demand for benefits must fall. That will not necessarily lead to unjust hardships. A number of proposals, some controversial and perhaps unlikely to gain wide support, have been suggested to keep the system viable:

• *Keep workers on the job until 70.* Better health care and working conditions are keeping people younger. Yet the official beginning of old age—when a worker can retire on full Social Security and qualify for Medicare—is still 65.

Despite their fitness, Americans are quitting young. Nearly half of men between 61 and 64 are retired. One reason: Social Security lets a worker retire at 62 with 80 percent of full benefits.

Thanks to the Social Security reforms of 1983, the full-benefit age will inch upward in the next century. Someone who turns 26 in 1988 cannot get full benefits until 67. That's the right idea, but the pace is too slow. It means the officially old will constitute 18 percent of the population in 2030, as compared with 12 percent today.

The government should make 70 the eligibility age for the *first* of the boomers, today's 42-year-olds. That way, only 15 percent of the population would qualify for full benefits in 2030, easing the burden on working people. Shrinking early-retirement benefits also would help.

• *Give workers bigger tax breaks for funding their own retirement.* A typical worker who retired in 1987 at 65 will strike a bonanza. By collecting $583 a month, in four years he will recover everything he paid out. But today's young worker may never get his money back.

A good plan would be to restore tax deductions for individual retirement accounts (IRAs). Under the Tax Reform Act of 1986, workers who earn more than $35,000 a year and are covered by corporate pension plans can no longer deduct IRA contributions. Congress should reverse itself. And to boost IRA saving, the government should acknowledge the truth: today's workers will receive much leaner benefits than today's elderly.

• *Don't pay for nursing-home care through payroll taxes.* Medicare pays almost nothing for nursing-home treatment, which averages $22,000 a year. Retirees who can't afford such care can get help from Medicaid *if they qualify.* Although standards vary, in most states Medicaid patients are allowed to keep their house, but cannot have more than a few thousand dollars in assets.

Senior Citizens

To eliminate this cruel solution, lobbyists for senior citizens hope . . . to push through federal insurance providing "free" nursing-home care. But Alice Rivlin and Joshua Wiener, senior fellows at the Brookings Institution, say such a system would add 2.8 percent to the FICA tax—already 15.02 percent of the first $45,000 of an individual's earnings.

That is the wrong way to do it. Subsidies that do not require beneficiaries to pay at least some of the cost inflate the demand for care. And a new FICA tax would add to the burden of the baby boomers, who should be socking the money away for their own Golden Years.

One option is private nursing-home insurance. Rivlin and Wiener predict that 30 years down the road private insurance will cover one-third of the elderly.

The other two-thirds face a tougher choice. If they want to avoid

Ed Gamble. Reprinted with permission.

selling assets, they and their heirs may have to go along with higher inheritance taxes. The net worth of people over 65 is $2 trillion, and about five percent is passed on to heirs every year. Rep. Jim Moody (D., Wis.), former co-chairman of AGE, sees taxing those transfers as a logical way to pay for nursing-home care: "It's not fair to spend society's money to preserve assets for someone's children."

Generational Equity

None of these steps will ease the pain of dealing with the last bulge the baby boomers make. Today the United States spends 11 percent of the gross national product on health. That share will come to 15 percent by 2000 because of the rising cost of high-tech care. The biggest jump will come after 2026, when the first boomers reach 80. At that age, they become the "old old," who require the most intensive treatment.

The cost of caring for the elderly is an endless open frontier, with the issues that divide the generations becoming literally matters of life and death. In the search for generational equity, we are going to face some hard choices. We should address them now, rather than later.

146

a critical thinking activity

Distinguishing Between Fact and Opinion

This activity is designed to help the basic reading and thinking skill of distinguishing between fact and opinion. Consider the following statement: "Social Security was established in 1935 to replace the income elderly people lost when they retired." This is a fact which can be verified by many published sources. But consider this statement: "Social Security has made a tremendous contribution to the strengthening of the social, economic, political and moral life of our nation." This statement expresses an opinion about Social Security. Some people may have a different assessment of it.

When investigating controversial issues it is important that one be able to distinguish between statements of fact and statements of opinion. It is also important to recognize that not all statements of fact are true. They may appear to be true, but some are based on inaccurate or false information. For this activity, however, we are concerned with understanding the difference between those statements which appear to be factual and those which appear to be based primarily on opinion.

Many of the following statements are taken from viewpoints covered in this chapter. Consider each statement carefully. *Mark O for any statement you believe is an opinion or interpretation of facts. Mark F for any statement you consider a fact. Mark U if you are uncertain.*

If you are doing this activity as a member of a class or group, compare your answers to those of other class or group members. Be able to defend your answers. You may discover that others come to different conclusions than you. Listening to the reasons others present for their answers may give you valuable insights in distinguishing between fact and opinion.

O = opinion
F = fact
U = uncertain

147

1. In 1965 President Johnson won approval for the Medicare and Medicaid health insurance programs which are run by the Social Security Administration.

2. Under current law, divorced women who were married less than ten years receive no share of the credit for their ex-husband's earnings.

3. The problem with Social Security is not that it transfers too much income to the old, but that it doesn't transfer enough.

4. Compulsory retirement coverage makes sense because the community would otherwise have to support those who might voluntarily choose not to provide for their old age.

5. It's all right to cut Social Security, because the system will collapse anyway when the baby boomers retire.

6. Today 3.3 workers toil to support a single beneficiary.

7. Since the supply of Social Security contributors is not likely to rise, the demand for benefits must fall.

8. Nearly half of all men between ages 61 and 64 are retired.

9. Social Security does not cause federal deficits.

10. In 1969, President Johnson began including Social Security accounts in the general budget.

11. Social Security is not welfare; it is a substitute for earnings lost through retirement.

12. For most people, job opportunities diminish after age 62, and relatively few work past 65.

13. The elderly are well off because of their assets, especially homes, and the fact that they no longer have expenses associated with employment.

14. Expenditures for the elderly at all levels of government exceed the amount spent on children, age seventeen and under, by more than three to one.

15. Reasons for the disparate treatment of the old and the young include the simple fact that elders vote and children do not.

16. A hundred years ago when Chancellor Bismarck in Germany established the first social insurance system, he set the retirement age at 65 because only a small minority reached that age.

Periodical Bibliography

The following articles have been selected to supplement the diverse views presented in this chapter.

Gary Stanley Becker	"Social Security Should Benefit Only the Elderly Poor," *Business Week*, January 16, 1989.
Stephen Chapman	"Off the Respirator," *The New Republic*, June 16, 1986.
Jean Cobb and Peter Montgomery	"Social Security: Is It Ripe for Reform?" *Common Cause Magazine*, January/February 1988.
Ernest Conine	"Before Cuts, Pierce Myths on Social Security," *Los Angeles Times*, December 21, 1988.
Susan Dentzer	"Social Security's Big Fix," *U.S. News & World Report*, December 26, 1988/January 2, 1989.
Edward Giltenan	"Social Security: The Bottom Line," *Forbes*, January 23, 1989.
Christine Gorman	"The $12 Trillion Temptation," *Time*, July 4, 1988.
Dorcas R. Hardy	"Social Security's Insecure Future," *The Wall Street Journal*, August 21, 1989.
Mickey Kaus	"Watch What You Call Welfare," *The Washington Monthly*, March 1989.
Robert Kuttner	"Flawed Fixes," *The New Republic*, January 6-13, 1986.
Paul Magnusson	"We Are Plundering the Social Security Till," *Business Week*, July 18, 1988.
The New Republic	"An Exchange on Social Security," May 18, 1987.
Jane Bryant Quinn	"Spending the Old-Age Fund," *Newsweek*, July 18, 1988.
Jeff A. Schnepper	"A Long-Term Solution for Social Security," *USA Today*, March 1989.
Lee Smith	"Trim That Social Security Surplus," *Fortune*, August 29, 1988.

How Should Society Meet the Elderly's Health Care Needs?

Chapter Preface

U.S. News & World Report has forecast the cost of one year of care in a nursing home would increase from $26,054 in 1988 to $158,275 in 2020. Shocking predictions like these have prompted health care experts to ask whether society must ration health care for the elderly.

Many experts, including The Hastings Center's Daniel Callahan, believe that spending large amounts of money on the elderly is foolhardy and unethical. In his 1987 book *Setting Limits*, Callahan argues that the U.S. overspends on health care for the elderly, especially for those over the age of 85. Callahan advocates concentrating more money and more scarce medical resources on younger generations.

Callahan's critics, including business expert Amitai Etzioni and health services professor Alan Sager, contend that rationing medical care for the elderly is immoral and discriminatory. They believe the elderly deserve full access to unlimited medical care.

The controversy over the rationing of health care fuels the debates in this chapter.

"Current government attempts not only fail to contain Medicare spending; they create financial incentives to give patients less care. This is unacceptable."

The Elderly Should Be Guaranteed Full Access to Health Care

Alan Sager

Alan Sager is an associate professor of health services at Boston University School of Public Health in the University's School of Medicine. In the following viewpoint, Sager argues that the high cost of health care prevents the elderly from getting the medical attention they need. Sager argues that Medicare exacerbates this problem. While Medicare reimbursement for services has remained stable, costs have risen dramatically. He advocates a national health insurance policy to guarantee quality care to everyone.

As you read, consider the following questions:

1. According to the author, how have medical costs affected the elderly?
2. What does Sager offer as an alternative to the current Medicare program?
3. What role have physicians and health care organizations played in the elderly's exclusion from health care, according to Sager?

Alan Sager, "Condition: Critical," *Dollars & Sense*, January/February 1988. Reprinted by permission of Dollars & Sense, 1 Summer Street, Somerville, Massachusetts 02143.

As they near retirement, most older Americans expect Medicare to pay their health care bills. They are soon disappointed. Medicare's hospital and physician benefits leave large gaps, and the program provides almost no coverage for the costs of medications or long-term care.

Older Americans pay about a quarter of their health care bills out of their own pockets—an average of $1,700 each year. Indeed, the average older American now pays 15% of his or her income for health care—as great a share as before Medicare was legislated.

Prohibitive Costs

Lower income citizens and those who suffer costly illnesses or disabilities must pay an even higher share. For many, the costs are prohibitive—and so these citizens go without care. A recent report indicates that low-income older citizens use 20% less physician and hospital care than the average older American. This figure probably understates the problem of underservice, since the poor are typically in greater need of care.

Gaps in Medicare coverage and high out-of-pocket costs are not older Americans' only health care problems. Many have trouble finding a sympathetic primary care physician willing to take the time to listen, diagnose, and provide thoughtful counsel. Without good primary care, other services (specialist physician, hospital, and long-term care) are often poorly coordinated.

Surprisingly, the problem with the U.S. health care system is not lack of money. Our 1987 bill for health care was $500 billion, over one-third more than for defense. Our total health care spending is greater than any other nation's, both in dollars per capita and as a share of GNP [gross national product]. Yet all other industrial democracies provide health care coverage to each of their citizens. People in these other nations are healthier as a result, enjoying greater longevity and lower infant mortality.

We already spend enough to guarantee health care for all, regardless of ability to pay. How can such high spending provide such inadequate protection, particularly for the older citizens who need it so badly?

Partial Protection

Almost one of every three U.S. health dollars benefits the 11% of our citizens aged 65 and above. This apparent imbalance actually makes sense, because older people need more care. Medicare, the main health program for elders, spent $68 billion in 1987 to cover 29 million older citizens.

Virtually all Americans aged 65 and over who receive social security are covered by Medicare's two distinct programs. Part A finances inpatient hospital care, while Part B covers physician services. Both are costly to the patient.

In Part A, the patient must pay a $540 deductible (set at the national average Medicare hospital cost per day) for each hospital admission. This deductible has nearly doubled between 1982 and 1987. For low- and moderate-income older Americans, it creates a substantial barrier to using hospital services.

Limited Benefits

Medicare's Part A also covers very limited, short-term convalescent nursing home and home health care services. Both require patients to make out-of-pocket co-payments for each nursing home day or home health visit. The existence of these benefits, however limited, leads many older citizens to believe that Medicare provides meaningful coverage of nursing home and home care costs. It does not. Medicare pays only about 2% of the national nursing home bill.

Coverage for physician services, through Medicare's Part B, is incomplete. Under Part B, after the patient meets an annual deductible of $75, Medicare pays up to 80% of allowable physician charges. The patient must pay the remaining 20%. If the physician chooses to charge a fee above what Medicare allows, the physician may recover this additional sum from the patient. (Only in Massachusetts is this practice, called "balance billing," now banned. Other states are contemplating action.) Older citizens enrolled in Part B also pay a monthly premium, which has been raised 37% to $24.80.

Citizens' Rights

No just society can deny the right of its citizens to the health care they need. We are the only industrial society that does.

Joseph Califano, quoted in *America*, March 7, 1987.

The financing for Part B is somewhat more progressive than that for Part A. Part A benefits are financed mainly by employed workers, through part of the social security tax (FICA) on all earned income up to a certain amount ($45,000 in 1988). Part B is financed from patient premiums and from general federal revenues. . . .

Containing Costs, Cutting Care

Despite prohibitively high health expenses for older citizens, legislators have focused their attention on cutting government, not patient, spending. In so doing, policymakers have exacerbated the problems facing elders while missing the real causes of the high costs of health care.

Health care costs are skyrocketing because of several factors built into the Medicare financing system. Medicare's methods of entitling individual citizens and paying physicians and hospitals have contributed to the cost explosion.

Medicare provides open-ended individual entitlement. Because physicians and hospitals are reimbursed for the care they deliver, they tend to decide what care an individual patient needs without considering either a budget limit or the needs of other patients. The result is skyrocketing expenditures on sometimes ineffective and expensive—but highly remunerative—high technology care for those who can afford the co-payments, and underfunding of treatments for more mundane problems. In short, the result is high costs and poor coverage.

Administrative costs are high because every case creates its own paper trail. Individual entitlement, complicated out-of-pocket payment schemes, and high financial barriers to access engender enormous administrative waste. By some estimates, a simpler administrative system, based on the British or Canadian health programs, could save as much as $25 to $40 billion annually.

Financial Barriers

In practice, entitlement is not open-ended at all, but is constrained by the patient's ability to pay. To reduce the government's Medicare expenditures, Congress added the financial barriers of deductibles and co-payments to restrain citizens from using benefits. As a result, many older citizens go without care while others impoverish themselves to get the care they need.

Medicare's physician reimbursement system is also wasteful. Medicare pays physicians by the traditional fee-for-service (or piece rate) method. This means that the more care physicians give, the more they are paid. As a result, physicians who seek to inflate their incomes often provide unnecessary and expensive care.

Medicare's fee schedules also drive up costs by favoring specialists. Primary care physicians who listen and diagnose are often badly underpaid relative to specialists. This helps explain the disproportionate number of specialists in the United States compared with other industrial democracies. The result is the costly over-provision of expensive treatments such as coronary artery bypass grafts and the relative neglect of chronic disabilities.

Medicare also reimbursed hospitals' costs. This practice, resembling the Defense Department's cost-plus relations with many of its contractors, provided no incentive to economize. More admissions—and more expensive operations—meant higher revenues.

Spending control has recently become an obsession to administrators of Medicare and other health programs. The most recent attempt to limit Medicare's obligations is the introduction of the diagnosis related group (DRG) system of prospective payment for hospital care. Each patient discharged from a hospital is assigned one of 470 DRG codes based on his or her illness. Medicare then pays hospitals a fixed sum for each patient based on the standardized price for the patient's DRG. If hospitals can provide care for less than the DRG payment, they get to keep the savings. If the care costs more, the hospitals absorb the difference.

Medical Nazism

I'm worried that a created "age limit" on medical care borders on Nazism. If we have an age limit on medical care, how long before we have an I.Q. limit, a social and educational class limit, etc.? A bag person has just as much right to adequate medical care as a business executive. And the poor and elderly are no less worthy of first-rate care than the young, educated, and well to do.

Reprinted with permission from *U.S. Catholic*, published by Claretian Publications, 205 West Monroe Street, Chicago, Illinois 60606.

While hospital profits on Medicare patients have increased under the DRG system, patient care has suffered. Hospitals now have the incentive to give less care. Costs have gone down somewhat, but not mainly through improved management efficiency. Savings have come from poorly planned staffing cuts, wage freezes, and other shortsighted actions. Hospitals have also sought patients who are less expensive to serve, a practice called "creaming."

Senior groups charge that because of DRGs, hospitals are discharging patients "quicker and sicker" and substituting less convenient (but better-paying) pre-admission testing for in-hospital services. To make matters worse, just when DRGs gave hospitals incentives to discharge patients sooner, Medicare administrators enacted miserly regulations discouraging home health agencies from meeting the increased need for post-hospital care.

Government attempts to limit Medicare payments to physicians have been unsuccessful. To control payments to physicians, Medicare capped increases in fees. Physicians responded by providing more marginally necessary services, and by "unbundling" —charging separately for services that had formerly been provided as a package. These are two forms of "gaming," or manipulating a payment system. Medicare payments rose rapidly despite the fee cap.

The Elderly and HMOs

Despairing of the possibility of cost control under fee-for-service, many . . . favor enrolling more older citizens in health maintenance organizations (HMOs). Medicare pays HMOs fixed monthly payments per enrolled and the HMO must provide all Medicare services.

With the right motivation, HMOs can provide more comprehensive care at lower costs. If HMO physicians are salaried, they are no longer rewarded for providing more care. But some HMOs (so far, not those serving Medicare patients) have sought to contain their costs by giving physicians sharp financial incentives to provide less care. For example, some HMO physicians make more money if they hospitalize fewer patients. . . .

Putting Patients First

Since overall funding for health care in the United States is already adequate, the challenge is to design a mechanism to spend our money better. As we strive to reform the U.S. health care system, we should keep several basic principles in mind.

First, all citizens should be equally entitled to all necessary health care. They should face no out-of-pocket costs when they seek health care. Money should be raised in the only fair way, through progressive taxation. Quality of care should not depend on ability to pay. No older Americans should be forced to impoverish themselves to receive care.

Second, all physicians and other professionals should be made financially neutral. That is, their incomes should not rise or fall with the amount of care their patients receive. Only then will government and patients be fully able to trust physicians.

Third, hospitals and other health care providers should work within limited annual budgets. These providers must then bear the burden of providing defined benefits to everyone. With limited budgets, trade-offs will always be necessary. Today, physicians and hospital administrators pretend that individual entitlement permits unlimited universal care. In practice, care is rationed by ability to pay. Priorities must be set democratically. Community representatives, patient advocates, organized workers, and other affected parties—not just physicians and hospital administrators—should make the difficult decisions about how to allocate limited resources.

Lastly, patients should enjoy freedom of choice among caregivers. This encourages hospitals, physicians, and other caregivers to be attentive to patients' wants. Caregivers should compete not by price but by scope of service, attentiveness, and compassion.

Current government attempts not only fail to contain Medicare spending; they create financial incentives to give patients less care. This is unacceptable. It is also unnecessary. Older Americans clearly deserve better.

"America's elderly have become an intolerable burden on the economic system and the younger generation's future."

The Elderly Cannot Be Guaranteed Full Access to Health Care

Richard D. Lamm

In the following viewpoint, Richard D. Lamm asserts that the elderly receive too much health care. According to Lamm, health care costs for the elderly eclipse the needs of the younger generations and foster resentment between the generations. Part I of the following viewpoint is an editorial writen by Lamm. Part II was taken from Lamm's book *Megatraumas*, written in 1985. Lamm, a former governor of Colorado, currently directs the Center for Public Policy and Contemporary Issues at the University of Denver.

As you read, consider the following questions:

1. What does Lamm predict will happen to health care for the elderly by the year 2000?
2. How does Lamm propose to reduce health care costs?
3. According to the author, what should be the prevailing attitude toward health care?

Richard D. Lamm, "Saving a Few, Sacrificing Many—at Great Cost," *The New York Times*, August 2, 1989. Copyright 1989 by The New York Times Company. Reprinted by permission. Excerpts from MEGATRAUMAS by Richard D. Lamm. Copyright © 1985 by Richard D. Lamm. Reprinted with permission of Houghton Mifflin Company.

I

The ancient Greeks observed that "to know all to ask is to know half." The cost of our inefficient health care system cannot continue to grow at more than twice the rate of inflation. Heretical questions must be asked.

Intensive Care

"What chance is there that she will leave this unit alive?" The group of doctors look annoyed at my question. We were clustered around the bed of a 91-year-old woman in the intensive care unit of a university hospital. She had been in intensive care for two weeks, kept alive by a web of tubes and hoses. The attending physician swallowed her personal resentment. "Very small, but every once in a while someone survives," she said. "Medicine must do everything possible as long as there is a chance."

America has approximately 87,000 intensive care beds, far more than any other country. An intensive care bed is the most expensive medical setting possible, usually staffed by one to one and one-half nurses per bed and surrounded by hundreds of thousands of dollars of high-technology equipment. They *do* save some people who would have been previously lost, but at a very high cost. They are thus symbolic of both our caring and our priorities.

Once people get into the health care system, we will spend fantastic amounts exploring a small chance of survival for them, yet 31 million Americans do not have basic health insurance and 30 percent of the kids in America have never seen a dentist. We have seemingly unlimited resources for patients in the system but painfully few for citizens outside the system. Our health care spending is reactive and reflexive rather than reflective.

Thirteen percent of our patients, many of them terminal, account for more than 50 percent of our hospital costs, yet Medicaid covers only 40 percent of the people living in poverty and a million American families have one or more members denied health care yearly. Almost 60 percent of Medicare's inpatient expenditures is spent on 12 percent of the recipients, too often for marginal procedures.

Economic Alarm

In one corner of the hospital, we are squeezing a few more days of pain-racked existence out of people for whom there is clearly no happy outcome; yet 600,000 women gave birth in 1988 with little or no prenatal care.

A hospital alarm goes off and the team rushes to resuscitate a man with prostate cancer. But an alarm has also gone off in our economy, and we ignore it at our peril.

We have among the lowest rates of investment in new plant and equipment in the industrialized world, yet there is a group of our brightest men and women using expensive Japanese machines and large amounts of our limited resources on frail bodies, many of whom everyone concedes will never leave this unit. On this day four of the 12 people in the unit have virtually no chance of leaving the hospital.

The Long Run

What matters most to me is that, as a community of the old and the young, we begin to think about where we want to go in the long run in our use of medicine to address the decline and death that have been the ineradicable marks of human aging. We have so far simply tried to use medicine to vanquish them or to keep them at bay as long as possible. That direction is no longer tenable. It is incoherent at its core and increasingly unworkable socially and economically.

Daniel Callahan, *Setting Limits,*, 1987.

In practically every town in America, the best building is the hospital (40 percent empty) and the worst a school (usually over-crowded). The highest paid professionals are doctors; the lowest paid professionals are teachers. We are overtreating our sick and undereducating our kids. We spend more than other industrialized nations on health care, both in total dollars and percent of gross national product devoted to health care, yet we do not keep our citizens as healthy as they do.

American Medicine

The basic dilemma of American medicine is that we have invented more health care than we can afford to pay for, and yet we find it terribly hard to set priorities. We rush to rescue people in intensive care units today whom just yesterday we abandoned. We spend too much money on high-technology care for a few and too little on basic health care for the many.

There is a permanently unconscious woman in Washington, D.C., maintained on an artificial life support system who became comatose and vegetative in 1953. We have spent millions keeping her heart beating in a city whose infant-mortality rate exceeds that of many third world countries.

A Fiscal Black Hole

Health care in America has become a fiscal black hole that can absorb unlimited resources. We have the finest technological means in the world, but all too few are asking, "To what end?" But another alarm sounds in the hospital's intensive care unit, and we must be off on our mission of "mercy."

II

Editor's note: The following section is in the form of a hypothetical memo to the U.S. President, dated January 2000.

America's elderly have become an intolerable burden on the economic system and the younger generation's future. In the name of compassion for the elderly, we have handcuffed the young, mortgaged their future, and drastically limited their hopes and aspirations.

Succeeding Generations

The policymakers of the 1960s and 1970s devised themselves golden parachute retirement programs and placed the cost in succeeding generations. They bought themselves homes with low interest rates and pay off those cheap loans with inflated dollars. They set up unsustainable pension systems—in government, in Social Security, and in many cases in private industry, and then they indexed them from the inflation that followed from their own excesses. They placed the bill for all these programs on succeeding generations, who consequently inherited the crippled economy their excesses caused. With a smile and grandfatherly advice, we tell the young to pay for our elderly's Social Security, military pensions, veterans' benefits, Medicare, nursing homes, and so forth. So what if both young parents have to work to support these systems and still earn a living? So what if grandchildren have to suffer because of our overgenerous and unsustainable programs for the elderly? The biblical story of the prodigal son has been turned on its head: we now have the sad but true story of the ''prodigal father.''

It is easy to see how this problem has developed. In 1970, 20 million Americans were over sixty-five years of age; by 1985, the number had risen to 29.5 million; today it is 39 million. They will number at least 55 million by 2031.

People over sixty-five in 1900 made up 4 percent of the population. It was 12 percent in 1985 and it is 17 percent today. And it is those in this category who vote in the heaviest numbers.

The problem is not going to get any easier. It is estimated that by the year 2040 nearly 20 percent of all Americans, some 50 million, will be sixty-five years or older, and we estimate that 40 percent of the federal budget will be devoted to them.

Runaway Health Care Costs

The increase in the number of aged, combined with our runaway health care costs, has given us the most expensive and fastest-rising aspect of the federal budget. Back in 1980, there were 105 million hospital patient days per year for persons age sixty-five and older; today there are 275 million such days. Adjusted for inflation, the costs of hospital care for the aged have tripled. The costs are not distributed evenly. It is estimated by Medicare that 7 percent of the people on Medicare receive an astonishing 67 percent of all Medicare costs. . . .

In 1950 only about half a million people in the United States were eighty-five or older, but today they number 5,136,000. In fifty years this old-old category has increased 900 percent. Very old women now outnumber very old men by five to two.

In 1980 one-quarter of the old-old were in nursing homes, and that percentage still holds. That means that we have built an average of one new nursing home for a hundred people *every* day from 1984 until today. That has been a staggering burden.

The incidence of dementing illnesses such as Alzheimer's disease roughly doubles every five years after age sixty-five. Thus, 1 percent of those sixty-five years old have a dementing illness; 2.5 percent of those age seventy; 5 percent of those age seventy-five; 12 percent of those age eighty; more than 20 percent of those between eighty-five and ninety; and 40 to 50 percent of those in their nineties. All other chronic diseases show up with increasing frequency.

Veterans are another elderly subgroup that has exploded in numbers. We now have nine million veterans over age sixty-five—three times the number there were in 1984. Two out of every three American men over sixty-five are veterans. We will spend $44.6 billion on military pensions in fiscal year 2000, compared to $1.2 billion spent in 1964.

Growing Resentment

The real crunch comes in the backlash we have been getting from current workers. These people are understandably growing resentful at the increasing burden placed upon them.

"The use of age as a principle for the allocation of resources can be perfectly valid."

Health Care for the Elderly Should Be Limited

Daniel Callahan

In the following viewpoint, Daniel Callahan argues that age is a legitimate way of determining who receives health care. According to Callahan, the elderly receive a disproportionate share of the health care in the U.S. He argues that this is shortsighted. Instead of spending money to treat people who will soon die, society should provide more basic health care to members of the younger generations, who have long lives ahead of them and can contribute to society. Callahan is the co-founder and director of The Hastings Center, a medical ethics think tank in Briarcliff Manor, New York.

As you read, consider the following questions:

1. How does Callahan justify restricting medical resources to the elderly?
2. Why does the author believe that limiting the elderly's health care is not discriminatory?
3. How would rationing medical treatment based on age affect the health care system in the U.S., according to Callahan?

Daniel Callahan, *Setting Limits*. New York: Simon & Schuster, 1987. Copyright © 1987 by Daniel Callahan. Reprinted by permission of SIMON & SCHUSTER, Inc.

Our common social obligation to the elderly is only to help them live out a natural life span; that is, the government is obliged to provide deliberately life-extending health care only to the age which is necessary to achieve that goal. Despite its widespread, almost universal rejection, I believe an age-based standard for the termination of life-extending treatment would be legitimate. Although economic pressures have put the question of health care for the elderly before the public eye, and constitute a serious issue, it is also part of my purpose to argue that, no less importantly, the meaning and significance of life for the elderly themselves is best founded on a sense of limits to health care. Even if we had unlimited resources, we would still be wise to establish boundaries. Our affluence and refusal to accept limits have led and allowed us to evade some deeper truths about the living of a good life and the place of aging and death in that life.

My underlying intention is to affirm the inestimable value of individual human life, of the old as much as the young, and the value of old age as part of our individual and collective life. I must then meet a severe challenge: to propose a way of limiting resources to the elderly, and a spirit behind that way, which are compatible with that affirmation. What does that affirmation mean in practice, and not merely in rhetoric? It means that individual human life is respected for its own sake, not for its social or economic benefits, and that individuals may not be deprived of life to serve the welfare, alleged or real, of others—individuals are not to be used to achieve the ends of others. To affirm the value of the aged is to continue according them every civil benefit and right acknowledged for other age groups unless it can be shown that their good is better achieved by some variation; to respect their past contributions when young and their present contributions now that they are old; and never, under any circumstances, to use their age as the occasion to demean or devalue them. That is the test my approach to allocation must meet. . . .

A Growing Problem

I have been working with the assumption that there is a growing problem of allocating health care to the elderly. There is enormous resistance to that idea. Is it true? As with any other definition of what is or is not a "problem," everything will depend on how we interpret the available evidence. . . .

Between 1965 and 1980, there was an increase in the life expectancy of those who reached age 65 from 14.6 to 16.4 years, with a projected increase by the year 2000 to 19.1 years. Between 1980 and 2040, a 41-percent general population increase is expected, but a 160-percent increase in those 65 or over. An increase of 27 percent in hospital days is expected for the general population by 2000, but a 42-percent increase for those 65 and over and a 91.2 percent increase for those 75 and over. The number of those 85 or older will go from 2.2 million in 1980 to 3.4 million in 1990 and 5.1 million in 2000; and those 65 and older from 25.5 million in 1980 to 31.7 million in 1990 and 35.0 million in 2000. Whereas in 1985 the elderly population of 11 percent consumed 29 percent of health-care expenditures, the expected 21-percent elderly population will consume 45 percent of such expenditures in 2040. The distinguished statistician Dorothy Rice, on summarizing the evidence, has written that "the number of very old people is increasing rapidly; the average period of diminished vigor will probably rise; chronic diseases will probably occupy a larger proportion of our life span, and the needs for medical care in later life are likely to increase substantially." . . .

Our Common Stake

The argument has been made, in effect, that there is no real problem of allocation of resources to the elderly for two important reasons. The first is that because everyone either is already old or will become old, a social policy of expenditures on the elderly benefits all generations in the long run; that is our "common stake." Second, health-care benefits for the aged have some immediate value for younger generations. They help relieve the young of burdens of care for the elderly they would otherwise have to bear. Research on those diseases which particularly affect the elderly has the side benefit of frequently producing health knowledge of pertinence to the young and their diseases. It also promises the young relief, when they are old, from diseases which they would otherwise be forced to anticipate. They are reassured about their own future to a greater extent. . . .

Rationing by Age

There are conditions under which a health-care system that rationed life-extending resources by age would be the prudent choice and therefore the choice that constituted a just or fair distribution of resources between age groups.

Norman Daniels, *Am I My Parents' Keeper?*, 1988.

I have considered responses pertinent to the contention that there is a need to ration health care for the elderly; while each of them has a certain plausibility, none is wholly convincing: It is possible and necessary to generalize about the elderly. It is possible that benefits to the aged will not automatically benefit other age groups. It is not premature to take the idea of rationing seriously. It is not a mistake to consider limitations on health care for the elderly even if there continue to be other social expenditures that we individually think wasteful. And it is more wishful thinking than anything else to believe that more efficient care of the elderly dying could save vast amounts of money. All those objections reflect a laudable desire to avoid any future policies that would require limiting benefits to the aging and that would use age as a standard for that limitation. They also betray a wish that economic realities would be happily coincidental with a commitment to the unrestricted good of the elderly. That may no longer be possible. A carefully drawn, widely discussed allocation policy is likely to be one safer in the long run for the elderly than the kind of ad hoc rationing (such as increased cost-sharing under Medicare) now present and increasing. . . .

The needs of the aged would be based on a general and socially established ideal of old age and not exclusively, as at present, on individual desires—even the widespread desire to live a longer life. That standard would make possible an allocation of resources to the aged which rested upon criteria that were at once age-based (aiming to achieve a natural life span) and need-based (sensitive to the differing health needs of individuals in achieving that goal). A fair basis for limits to health care for the aged would be established, making a clear use of age as a standard, but also recognizing the heterogeneity of the needs of the old within those limits. . . .

Age or Need?

The use of age as a principle for the allocation of resources can be perfectly valid. I believe it is a necessary and legitimate basis for providing health care to the elderly. It is a necessary basis because there is not likely to be any better or less arbitrary criterion for the limiting of resources in the face of the open-ended possibilities of medical advancement in therapy for the aged. Medical "need" can no longer work as an allocation principle; it is too elastic a concept. Age is a legitimate basis because it is a meaningful and universal category. It can be understood at the level of common sense, can be made relatively clear for policy purposes, and can ultimately be of value to the aged themselves if combined with an ideal of old age that focuses on its quality rather than its indefinite extension.

This may be a most distasteful proposal for many of those trying to combat ageist stereotypes and to protect the deepest interests of the elderly. The main currents of gerontology (with the tacit support of medical tradition) have moved in the opposite direction, toward stressing individual needs and the heterogeneity of the elderly. That emphasis has already led to a serious exploration of the possibility of shifting some old-age entitlement programs from an age to a need basis. . . .

My principle of age-based rationing is not founded on the demeaning idea of measuring "productivity" in the elderly. The use of age as a standard treats everyone alike, aiming that each will achieve a natural life span, productive or not. Far from tolerating social abandonment, it will aim at improving care for the elderly, though not life-extending care. A standard of allocation rooted not in dehumanizing calculations of the economic value or productivity of the elderly, but in a recognition that beyond a certain point they will already have had their fair share of resources does not degrade the elderly or lessen the value of their lives. It is only a way of recognizing that the generations pass and that death must come to us all. Nor does it demean the aged as individuals, or signal indifference to the variations among them, to note that they share the trait of being old. It is only if society more generally devalues the aged for being aged—by failing, most notably, to provide the possibility of inherent meaning and significance in old age (as is the case with the modernizing project)—that their individual lives are treated as less valuable. There is nothing unfair about using age as a category if the purpose of doing so is to achieve equity between the generations, to give the aged their due in living out a life-span opportunity range, and to emphasize that the distinctive place and merits of old age are not nullified by aging and death.

The Right Motives

That a society could be mature enough to limit care for the aged with no diminution of respect, or could recognize the claims of other age groups without an implication that the elderly are less valuable than they are, seems rarely to be considered. By contrast, the motives I have been advancing reject not the elderly, but a notion of the good of the elderly based on pretending that death and old age can be overcome or ignored, that life has value only if it continues indefinitely, and that there is nothing to be said for the inherent value and contributions of the elderly as elderly. A society that adopts a wholly modernizing approach to old age must necessarily find the possibility of any limitation on care for the elderly a threat. It has robbed old age of all redeeming significance, and only constant efforts to overcome it are acceptable. To pick on the aged for "bureaucratic parsimony," to use Mark Siegler's term, would surely be wrong if done because they were perceived as weak and defenseless, a nice target-of-opportunity for cost containment. That is a very different matter from a societal decision that the overall welfare of the generations, the proper function of medicine, and a fitting understanding of old age and death as part of the life cycle justify limitation on some forms of medical care for the elderly.

"A policy that would stop Federal support for certain kinds of care . . . would halt treatment for the aged, poor, the near-poor, . . . while the rich would continue to buy all the care they wished to."

Health Care for the Elderly Should Not Be Limited

Amitai Etzioni

Amitai Etzioni is a visiting professor at the Harvard Business School in Cambridge, Massachusetts. In the following viewpoint, Etzioni contends that rationing health care resources by age would be the first step in discriminating against the elderly.

As you read, consider the following questions:

1. How could limiting health care for the elderly endanger other people, according to the author?
2. Why does the author believe the elderly should receive all the health care they need?
3. According to Etzioni, how much health care do the elderly really use?

Amitai Etzioni, "Spare the Old, Save the Young," *The Nation*, June 11, 1988. Copyright © 1988 by The Nation Company, Inc.

In the coming years, Daniel Callahan's call to ration health care for the elderly, put forth in his book *Setting Limits*, is likely to have a growing appeal. Practically all economic observers expect the United States to go through a difficult time as it attempts to work its way out of its domestic (budgetary) and international (trade) deficits. Practically every serious analyst realizes that such an endeavor will initially entail slower growth, if not an outright cut in our standard of living, in order to release resources to these priorities. When the national economic "pie" grows more slowly, let alone contracts, the fight over how to divide it up intensifies. The elderly make an especially inviting target because they have been taking a growing slice of the resources (at least those dedicated to health care) and are expected to take even more in the future. Old people are widely held to be "nonproductive" and to constitute a growing "burden" on an ever-smaller proportion of society that is young and working. Also, the elderly are viewed as politically well-organized and powerful; hence "their" programs, especially Social Security and Medicare, have largely escaped the Reagan attempts to scale back social expenditures, while those aimed at other groups—especially the young, but even more so future generations—have been generally curtailed. There are now some signs that a backlash may be forming.

Generation War

If a war between the generations, like that between the races and between the genders, does break out, historians may accord former Governor Richard Lamm of Colorado the dubious honor of having fired the opening shot in his statement that the elderly ill have "got a duty to die and get out of the way." Phillip Longman, in his book *Born to Pay*, sounded an early alarm. However, the historians may well say, it was left to Daniel Callahan, a social philosopher and ethicist, to provide a detailed rationale and blueprint for limiting the care to the elderly, explicitly in order to free resources for the young. Callahan's thesis deserves close examination because he attempts to deal with the numerous objections his approach raises. If his thesis does not hold, the champions of limiting funds available to the old may have a long wait before they will find a new set of arguments on their behalf.

In order to free up economic resources for the young, Callahan offers the older generation a deal: Trade quantity for quality; the elderly should not be given life-*extending* services but better years while alive. Instead of the relentless attempt to push death to an older age, Callahan would stop all development of life-extending technologies and prohibit the use of ones at hand for those who outlive their "natural" life span, say, the age of 75. At the same time, the old would be granted more palliative medicine (e.g., pain

169

killers) and more nursing-home and home-health care, to make their natural years more comfortable.

Callahan's call to break an existing ethical taboo and replace it with another raises the problem known among ethicists and sociologists as the "slippery slope." Once the precept that one should do "all one can" to avert death is given up, and attempts are made to fix a specific age for a full life, why stop there? If, for instance, the American economy experiences hard times in the 1990s, should the "maximum" age be reduced to 72, 65—or lower? And should the care for other so-called unproductive groups be cut off, even if they are even younger? Should countries that are economically worse off than the United States set their limit, say, at 55?

Moral Implications

The major flaw is Callahan's total neglect of the moral implications of singling out any group of Americans as not worthy of life-extending care. What impact would such a policy have on the moral fabric of American society? What group might be singled out next as undesirable, burdensome, and costly? If the aged can become vulnerable through scapegoating, who among us is next in line?

Robert H. Binstock, *The World & I*, December 1988.

This is not an idle thought, because the idea of limiting the care the elderly receive in itself represents a partial slide down such a slope. Originally, Callahan, the Hastings Center (which he directs) and other think tanks played an important role in re-defining the concept of death. Death used to be seen by the public at large as occurring when the lungs stopped functioning and, above all, the heart stopped beating. In numerous old movies and novels, those attending the dying would hold a mirror to their faces to see if it fogged over, or put an ear to their chests to see if the heart had stopped. However, high technology made these criteria obsolete by mechanically ventilating people and keeping their hearts pumping. Hastings et al. led the way to provide a new technological definition of death: brain death. Increasingly this has been accepted, both in the medical community and by the public at large, as the point of demise, the point at which care should stop even if it means turning off life-extending machines, because people who are brain dead do not regain consciousness. At the same time, most doctors and a majority of the public as well continue strongly to oppose terminating care to people who are conscious, even if there is little prospect for recovery, despite considerable debate about certain special cases.

Callahan now suggests turning off life-extending technology for all those above a certain age, even if they could recover their full human capacity if treated. It is instructive to look at the list of technologies he would withhold: mechanical ventilation, artificial resuscitation, antibiotics and artificial nutrition and hydration. Note that while several of these are used to maintain brain-dead bodies, they are also used for individuals who are temporarily incapacitated but able to recover fully; indeed, they are used to save young lives, say, after a car accident. But there is no way to stop the development of such new technologies and the improvement of existing ones without depriving the young of benefit as well. (Antibiotics are on the list because of an imminent "high cost" technological advance—administering them with a pump implanted in the body, which makes their introduction more reliable and better distributes dosages.)

One may say that this is Callahan's particular list; other lists may well be drawn. But any of them would start us down the slope, because the savings that are achieved by turning off the machines that keep brain-dead people alive are minimal compared with those that would result from the measures sought by the people calling for new equity between the generations. And any significant foray into deliberately withholding medical care for those who can recover does raise the question, Once society has embarked on such a slope, where will it stop?

Age Limits

Those opposed to Callahan, Lamm and the other advocates of limiting care to the old, but who also favor extending the frontier of life, must answer the question, Where will the resources come from? One answer is found in the realization that defining people as old at the age of 65 is obsolescent. That age limit was set generations ago, before changes in life styles and medicines much extended not only life but also the number and quality of productive years. One might recognize that many of the "elderly" can contribute to society not merely by providing love, companionship and wisdom to the young but also by continuing to work, in the traditional sense of the term. Indeed, many already work in the underground economy because of the large penalty—a cut in Social Security benefits—exacted from them if they hold a job "on the books."

Allowing elderly people to retain their Social Security benefits while working, typically part-time, would immediately raise significant tax revenues, dramatically change the much-feared dependency-to-dependent ratio, provide a much-needed source of child-care workers and increase contributions to Social Security (under the assumption that anybody who will continue to work will continue to contribute to the program). There is also evidence that people who continue to have meaningful work will live longer and healthier lives, without requiring more health care, because psychic well-being in our society is so deeply associated with meaningful work. Other policy changes, such as deferring retirement, modifying Social Security benefits by a small, gradual stretching out of the age of full-benefit entitlement, plus some other shifts under way, could be used readily to gain more resources. Such changes might be justified prima facie because as we extend life and its quality, the payouts to the old may also be stretched out.

Beyond the question of whether to cut care or stretch out Social Security payouts, policies that seek to promote intergenerational equity must be asssessed as to how they deal with another matter

Lisa Blackshear. Reprinted with permission.

of equity: that between the poor and the rich. A policy that would stop Federal support for certain kinds of care, as Callahan and others propose, would halt treatment for the aged, poor, the near-poor and even the less-well-off segment of the middle class (although for the latter at a later point), while the rich would continue to buy all the care they wished to. Callahan's suggestion that a consensus of doctors would stop certain kinds of care for all elderly people is quite impractical; for it to work, most if not all doctors would have to agree to participate. Even if this somehow happened, the rich would buy their services overseas either by going there or by importing the services. There is little enough we can do to significantly enhance economic equality. Do we want to exacerbate the inequalities that already exist by completely eliminating access to major categories of health care services for those who cannot afford to pay for them?

Slipping Down the Slope

In addition to concern about slipping down the slope of less (and less) care, the *way* the limitations are to be introduced raises a serious question. The advocates of changing the intergenerational allocation of resources favor rationing health care for the elderly but nothing else. This is a major intellectual weakness of their argument. There are other major targets to consider within health care, as well as other areas, which seem, at least by some criteria, much more inviting than terminating care to those above a certain age. Within the medical sector, for example, why not stop all interventions for which there is no hard evidence that they are beneficial? Say, public financing of psychotherapy and coronary bypass operations? Why not take the $2 billion or so from plastic surgery dedicated to face lifts, reducing behinds and the like? Or require that all burials be done by low-cost cremations rather than using high-cost coffins? . . .

Last but not least, as the United States enters a time of economic constraints, should we draw new lines of conflict or should we focus on matters that sustain our societal fabric? During the 1960s numerous groups gained in political consciousness and actively sought to address injustices done to them. The result has been some redress and an increase in the level of societal stress (witness the deeply troubled relationships between the genders). But these conflicts occurred in an affluent society and redressed deeply felt grievances. Are the young like blacks and women, except that they have not yet discovered their oppressors—a group whose consciousness should be raised, so it will rally and gain its due share?

The answer is in the eye of the beholder. There are no objective criteria that can be used here the way they can be used between the races or between the genders. While women and minorities have the same rights to the same jobs at the same pay

173

as white males, the needs of the young and the aged are so different that no simple criteria of equity come to mind. Thus, no one would argue that the teen-agers and those above 75 have the same need for schooling or nursing homes.

The Medical Establishment

Once such an arbitrary variable as age is allowed to be used by the government and the medical establishment to decide who shall receive "aggressive" medical care—then the door is open for such criteria as race, religion and social class to be similarly used.

Michael Klausner, *The Wall Street Journal*, February 24, 1988.

At the same time, it is easy to see that those who try to mobilize the young—led by a new Washington research group, Americans for Generational Equity (AGE), formed to fight for the needs of the younger generation—offer many arguments that do not hold. For instance, they often argue that today's young, age 35 or less, will pay for old people's Social Security, but by the time that they come of age they will not be able to collect, because Social Security will be bankrupt. However, this argument is based on extremely farfetched assumptions about the future. In effect, Social Security is now and for the foreseeable future overprovided, and its surplus is used to reduce deficits caused by other expenditures, such as Star Wars, in what is still an integrated budget. And, if Social Security runs into the red again somewhere after the year 2020, relatively small adjustments in premiums and payouts would restore it to financial health.

Above all, it is a dubious sociological achievement to foment conflict between the generations, because, unlike the minorities and the white majority, or men and women, many millions of Americans are neither young nor old but of intermediate ages. We should not avoid issues just because we face stressing times in an already strained society; but maybe we should declare a moratorium on raising new conflicts until more compelling arguments can be found in their favor, and more evidence that this particular line of divisiveness is called for.

174

> *"A new social insurance program for long-term care could deliberately build up reserves, just as if it were a private insurance plan."*

National Insurance Should Fund Long-Term Care

Robert Kuttner

Robert Kuttner is the economics editor of *The New Republic*, a weekly news and opinion journal. In the following viewpoint, Kuttner argues that the way to pay for long-term care for the elderly is for the government to set up a health care insurance plan similar to Social Security. The insurance plan would create revenue specifically for long-term care, which would preclude outrageous expenditures by either the government or the public.

As you read, consider the following questions:

1. How does Kuttner argue that his social insurance program will provide for long-term care?
2. According to Kuttner, how would his insurance plan affect the relationship between the elderly and younger generations?
3. What does the author hope to accomplish with the social insurance plan?

Robert Kuttner, "Uncle Bob's All-Purpose Tonic," *The New Republic*, September 12 & 19, 1988. Reprinted by permission of THE NEW REPUBLIC, © 1988, The New Republic, Inc.

The issue of long-term care for the elderly has forced its way onto the national agenda. The logic of social insurance to pay for nursing care and home care is very persuasive. But the cause is seemingly hopeless because of the familiar fiscal litany: Balancing the budget must take priority. Entitlements should be cut, not expanded. Old folks already get more than their fair share. Economic health requires a higher private savings rate before we contemplate additional social outlay. And so on.

Economic Growth

The savings rate argument is especially persuasive, since it is undeniable that the savings rates of nations are closely correlated to their rates of economic growth, and the United States has long had the lowest savings rate among the advanced economies. It declined from 7.1 percent in 1980 to just 3.7 percent in 1987.

Yet surprisingly, the very demand for a costly new social program opens the door to a fundamentally different way of financing social spending that would help the savings rate and the larger economy at the same time. The idea, paradoxically, is to use social insurance as a source of net savings for the economy. Like Social Security, which is now in surplus, a new social insurance program for long-term care could deliberately build up reserves, just as if it were a private insurance plan. The reserves would add to the economy's rate of savings. The same effect could be achieved through a major reform of private pensions—extending them to all employees and bringing them under more consistent public control. The common thread in both proposals is the idea that adequate money for America's collective retirement should be set aside in advance, raising the quality of services and the rate of collective savings simultaneously.

Of the various institutions that provide income and services for retirement—Social Security pensions, private pensions, Medicare, funds for nursing home care—only private pensions have served as a source of true savings, by building up funds sufficient to pay future claims. By contrast, the public pieces of the retirement system—Social Security, Medicare, and Medicaid (which pays for nursing home care)—have been operated as "pay-as-you-go" programs. Current taxes on today's working people finance current benefits paid out to today's retired people. No accumulation of savings takes place.

Social Security

However, the 1983 restructuring of Social Security set in motion a far-reaching change by deliberately building up a surplus in the Social Security accounts. The surplus, projected to peak in 2020 at $12 trillion, was devised in order to anticipate the greater-than-normal drain on Social Security that will occur when the baby boom generation begins retiring. Thus, for the first time under

Social Security, working-age people will be paying at least part of their own retirement costs in advance, just as if they were putting money in the bank. And the existence of a big Social Security surplus makes it respectable to contemplate advance-funding of the costs of old age as a general fiscal strategy.

In addition, there is a real ground swell of popular support for long-term care, both home care and nursing care. At present, Medicare does not cover nursing home stays, nor do most private health insurance plans. To qualify for nursing home care under Medicaid, middle-class people must first become welfare cases. Often a healthy spouse must also become a pauper, so that a wife or husband with Alzheimer's disease or some other debilitating illness can meet the welfare test for extended nursing care. Home care, an often superior alternative, falls between the policy cracks, because no major public program or private insurance policy re-imburses its costs. As a result, large numbers of old people who might remain in their own homes at a fraction of the cost to society are put into nursing homes.

It is convenient to dismiss this political tide as the artificial creation of a mob of prosperous elders, whipped into a frenzy by the American Association of Retired Persons. In truth, as any middle-aged American with an elderly parent appreciates, care for an aging population is a multigenerational concern. Several recent public opinion polls have identified long-term care for the elderly as voters' top priority for increased government spending, outranking aid to the homeless, education, environment, defense, and every other issue. The support is hardly surprising, for most of us will eventually get old. And as the population ages, it makes sense to set aside money for its care in advance.

Universal Coverage

While one of the better policies we found may be a reasonable choice for more affluent people who can qualify, millions of Americans will still be left without adequate coverage. The private insurance system cannot spread its costs over a large enough number of people to make coverage affordable for the millions who need it. Only the federal government can do that. Universal coverage for long-term care—whether the service is rendered at home or in a nursing facility—must be addressed.

Gail Shearer, quoted in *Public Citizen*, September/October 1988.

Another sign that long-term care has come of age is a volume by Alice Rivlin and Joshua Weiner, *Caring for the Disabled Elderly*. Rivlin, director of economic studies at the Brookings Institution, is former chief of the Congressional Budget Office, and something of a born-again fiscal conservative. In the mid-1980s she achieved notoriety as one of the first leading Democratic economists to place deficit reduction above all other social policy goals. The 1984 volume in Brookings's budget series "Economic Choices," the first under Rivlin's direction, called for a program of budget balance even more stringent than the Gramm-Rudman formula, including steep cuts in entitlements and new consumption taxes, leading the *Wall Street Journal* editorial page to crow, "Brookings Joins the Supply Side."

A Social Insurance Program

But if Rivlin's backing was a coup for conservatives in 1984, she is an even more surprising catch for liberals in 1988. Her book carefully evaluates all the alternatives and concludes there is no adequate alternative to a general social insurance program to provide nursing and home care. Rivlin and Weiner suggest that a comprehensive program would cost about $12 billion to $18 billion yearly in addition to costs now borne by Medicaid, which would be folded into a new program. Variations on the theme, proposed by Senator Ted Kennedy, Congressman Claude Pepper, and others, put the annual cost at around $20 billion.

The fiscal deficiency in the Kennedy, Pepper, and Rivlin approaches is that each in its own way raises taxes just enough to finance current payouts; no addition to net savings would occur. But if the program were designed to accumulate gradually a large surplus, on the model of a private insurance plan, there would be both an economic and a political benefit. Economically, the nation would be setting aside money for its old age and adding to the savings supply. Politically, wage earners would know that they were being taxed to pay for their own retirement years, and not just for today's "undeserving" elders. The argument is often heard that the young are already bearing too heavy a tax load to pay for the old. The remedy is to create a retirement system in which the young are setting aside funds for themselves.

Some say that tax-supported nursing care would tax everyone in order to allow people of means to pass their wealth along to their children, untouched by the expenses of old age. From that perspective, the present Medicaid-financed system of nursing care appeals, because it requires middle-class recipients of nursing home aid to deplete their own assets first. By analogy, it has been proposed that in any general program of long-term care, the government might bill the estates of people who consumed the care, after their demise. On reflection, however, it seems highly unjust that the heirs of people lucky enough not to need nursing care should collect untouched inheritances, while those whose parents or spouses required institutionalization should lose everything. The whole point of insurance is risk-sharing. If estates are to be tapped at all to pay for nursing care, it would be far more equitable to raise

178

general estate taxes to pay the costs of those with the misfortune to spend their last days in a nursing home.

The Reagan tax cut of 1981 raised the exemption from federal inheritance taxes to $600,000, costing the Treasury on the order of $10 billion a year. To the opinion-leader class, $600,000 sounds like a rather modest estate, but in fact only one percent of estates in 1987 met that test. If the tax threshold were lowered to $300,000, and tax rates on large estates raised, a small portion of the inheritances of the well-to-do would finance long-term care for everyone. There is no more defensible moment in the life cycle to justify redistributive taxation than at the time when the fortune of one generation is left to the next. Tapping estates to finance nursing care also addresses the "generational equity" concern, for it is a kind of post-mortem tax on the accumulated assets of the old to pay for the care of the old.

Comprehensive Benefits

An ideal program would be publicly financed by a payroll tax and would be uniform nationwide, although probably administered by the states. It would cover nursing home care at all levels and home care on an equal basis, and would include a state-administered screening program to help determine which patients need nursing home care and which could best be cared for in the community— taking social as well as medical factors into account. It would pay comprehensive benefits, putting a halt to the impoverishment of families by the cost of long-term care. And it would control nursing home payment rates and new bed construction tightly, to keep nursing home profits in line and the program financially viable.

Karen Erdman, *Public Citizen*, September/October 1988.

Advance-funded health care is only one source of social income that could also boost the collective savings rate. The other major source is the pension system, whose present form is inadequate both as a source of secure collective savings and of personal retirement income. As noted, pensions make up the one leg of the retirement income system that is currently advance-funded. Pension funds are now the principal source of new capital for the nation's capital markets, and they hold a prodigious $1.7 trillion in accumulated wealth. This form of collective savings has virtually supplanted private household savings. But a close look at the flaws in the private pension system offers a powerful argument in favor of a public, universal system.

Private pensions began early in this century as a management tool for rewarding long-service employees and for easing older workers out of the labor force. Gradually, private pensions have evolved into a system on which workers rely for part of their retire-

179

ment income and on which the economy depends for capital ac-cumulation. They are now partially regulated, and they consume about $40 billion in annual tax subsidies. But since employers are under no compulsion to provide pension plans, they are unreliable from the perspective of the employee and all but impossible to regulate effectively.

Only about half the nation's workers currently are enrolled in pension plans, and a plan may be terminated at the whim of the employer. Since 1980, when raiding of pension plans became widespread, management has taken some $18 billion out of pen-sion plans on the premise that they were "overfunded." (Over-funding is the result of manipulated actuarial assumptions or an inflated stock market.) An employee also bears the risk that a firm may go bankrupt, or that it may change hands, and the system owes him only the pension credits accumulated to date. Although the law now requires that pension credits be locked in ("vested") after five years of service, a worker who changes jobs frequently loses substantial savings supposedly accumulated on his behalf. Unlike Social Security, which is fully indexed, only about two per-cent of private pension plans have a cost-of-living adjustment for inflation. A worker who retired in, say 1973, is being paid in 1973 dollars and has lost more than half the value of his pension, even though the money that he paid into the fund during his working life is earning a return in 1988 dollars.

Optional Pension Plans

Because pension plans are optional (to the employer), the at-tempt to regulate them has been a hopeless cause. The Employee Retirement Income Security Act (ERISA) imposes convoluted regulations on pension fund trustees, yet fails to protect employees from a wide range of abuses, most notably the raiding and termina-tion of pension plans. Since 1980 the fraction of the work force covered by a pension plan has actually declined from 56 percent to 52 percent.

Yet earnings-related, contributory pensions remain a good idea, an important source of both capital and retirement income. The flaw in the current system is that the pension is tied to the in-dividual's employer rather than to his earnings history, and that the fund of capital is usually controlled by the employer. All of the abuses and regulatory headaches would disappear if the crazy quilt of private pension plans were collapsed into a single national pension system, which would be fully "portable," following workers from job to job, and under the control of public trustees. A second-best reform would be a fully portable pension plus a "play or pay" rule, under which all employers would have to set up a private pension plan or pay a tax into a public plan for un-covered workers, as President Carter's Commission on Pension

Policy recommended (with notably poor timing), in February 1981.

Like a system of advance-funded health care for the elderly, a universal pension system based on contributions and earnings history would increase the national savings rate and set aside real money for old age. The virtue of private systems of saving for retirement is not that they are private, but that they are advance-funded. But public systems can be advanced-funded too. The obstacles are mainly political, not economic. In the case of health care, there is predictable opposition from private insurers. In the case of pensions, there is a veritable pension/industrial complex ranging from actuaries to fund managers to large and small businesses that want the system to remain as it is.

Policy Questions

Beyond the purely self-interested opposition, however, there are some fair policy questions about the liabilites of a system of savings for social welfare and retirement. They include these:

Won't this approach at some point create an excessive savings rate? No, we should only be so lucky! The real issue is whether to try to increase savings rates Reagan-style, by inducing the already wealthy to amass more wealth, or to raise the savings rate in a distributively fairer manner that helps ordinary people. Reaganomics actually lowered the savings rate, because the Reagan budget deficit consumed private savings. A social savings approach would raise it. Some conceivable rate of savings, of course, would be excessive. But as this approach gradually increases our total savings rate, the government can compensate by running a more accommodative monetary policy, and can run moderate deficits in the current budget as periodic anti-recession medicine.

Won't advance-funding require even higher taxes than a new round of pay-as-you-go entitlements? Yes, certainly. But these taxes will increase the national savings rate and give working-age people full confidence in the safety net for their own old age. It's worth it. If we muster the political support for a new round of entitlements, we might as well do it right, in a way that helps the larger economy at the same time. Reforming inheritance taxes and raising the income ceiling on payroll taxes would produce most of the necessary money. A fallback alternative is a value-added tax.

Why not just rely on private insurance and private savings? Because most people don't make enough money to put aside sufficient funds for both living expenses and health emergencies in their retirement. Even when the government was bribing people to save, through Individual Retirement Accounts, only about seven percent of people with incomes below $20,000 a year and 18 percent of people earning $20,000 to $35,000 a year had IRA accounts. Moderate-income people, in general, are strapped to make ends meet. They don't save much. Also, private insurance raises the problem of what insurers delicately call "adverse selection," meaning that people most likely to incur costs have the effrontery to apply for the policy. With universal social insurance, there is no such problem.

Who will control the money in these new health and retirement trust funds? Public trustees. The money would be invested in government and corporate bonds, and in blue-chip stocks. Public trustees could hardly do worse than the current crop of pension funds managers, who churn their accounts, collect fat fees, and fail even to match the Dow Jones average performance. It is also an exquisite irony that pension funds are sometimes the fuel for the hostile takeovers that result in the termination of those funds. Public trustees would get pension funds out of the hostile takeover game. This new pool of social capital for blue-chip investments would also free up private capital to play a more entrepreneurial role, to which it is suited.

The Public Approach

Isn't this scheme rather collectivist? Indeed it is. But so are Social Security and Medicare, and so is the General Motors pension fund. All of them amass collective capital on behalf of individuals. The difference is that private pension funds keep pools of collective savings under arbitrary private control. They confuse the public policy goal of amassing retirement savings with narrow private goals of financing corporate takeovers or maximizing current corporate earnings, and they create capricious hardships for beneficiaries. The public approach cuts through a whole messy series of regulatory dilemmas, because it is collective, universal, and does not need to pit public goals against private ones.

To thrive as an economy, America must increase its savings rate. To thrive as a society, America must find the money to allow its citizens to live out their years in dignity. These goals need not be in conflict. At issue is whether we are willing to open the door to social savings, an approach that is superior in terms of both social equity and economic efficiency.

"The government's role should be to promote widespread use of long-term care insurance and other private financing mechanisms."

Private Citizens Should Fund Long-Term Care

Peter J. Ferrara

In the following viewpoint, the author, Peter J. Ferrara, argues that middle-class and wealthy people should buy private health insurance to provide for their long-term health care needs. Ferrara argues that the government can only afford to fund long-term care for the needy. Private insurance and other creative, private financing ideas can provide adequately for most people, contends the author. Ferrara is associate professor of law at George Mason University School of Law in Fairfax, Virginia.

As you read, consider the following questions:

1. What gaps in Medicare and Medicaid would private long-term care insurance fill, according to Ferrara?
2. What other private financing ideas does Ferrara suggest to supplement the insurance plan?
3. According to the author, how would the private long-term insurance work?

Peter J. Ferrara, excerpted from *A National Health System for the Elderly: Critical Issues*. Washington, D.C.: The Heritage Foundation, 1989. Reprinted by permission.

The elderly need and use medical services more than any other group of Americans. Often with a fixed income and a limited ability to earn more, they are especially vulnerable to rapidly rising medical and catastrophic health care expenses. The middle-class elderly fear particularly that the high costs of treating a severe or chronic illness could wipe out their life savings.

Social Insurance

Like several other countries, the United States has adopted a social insurance approach, in the form of Medicare, to deal with these fears of the elderly. But this social insurance approach does not solve the problem of high medical costs for America's elderly. They pay as much or more of their income for medical care as they did before Medicare was adopted. At the same time, the quality of care, in many respects, is deteriorating under federal cost control regulations. Medicare is still badly underfunded over the long run, and it will require huge payroll and income tax increases to maintain promised benefits. Workers already face heavy payroll tax burdens to pay for Medicare, which is consuming ever larger amounts of federal revenues. Expanding Medicare to cover additional costs, such as that of nursing home care, would aggravate the system's problems.

America deserves a system that enables all of its elderly citizens to obtain essential quality medical care without great financial hardship. To accomplish this, a new approach is needed, based on competition, market incentives, and greater consumer choice. . . .

While cost to the elderly of their Medicare coverage is going up, the quality of care they receive in certain respects seems to be going down, because of Medicare cost control regulations. In 1983, Congress adopted the Prospective Payment System (PPS) for Medicare. This system classifies all illnesses requiring hospital treatment into 475 categories (called Diagnostic Related Groups, or DRGs), and sets the amount it will pay under Medicare in each locality for treatment of the illness in each category. The set fees are supposed to be based on an average of local hospital charges for each illness. If the hospital can treat the patient for less than the set fee, it can keep the difference. If the treatment costs more, however, the hospital cannot collect the extra charges from the patient and must absorb the loss. . . .

Medicare also pays little for long-term care in nursing homes or other settings, and the program provides no coverage for dental care, hearing aids, eyeglasses, walking aids and similar items. These uncovered costs must be paid by the elderly themselves in addition to the program's deductible and coinsurance fees. Medicare, in fact, currently pays less than half of the medical expenses of retirees. . . .

Despite the problems of Medicare and the potential cost of expanding the social insurance system for such additional coverage as nursing home care, Americans understandably want action to address the mounting financial problems of many elderly afflicted with infirmity or ill health. For this, another major expansion of social insurance is not needed. Indeed, it would fail. The solution instead is a comprehensive approach based on the following central principles:

1) The government should help those Americans without sufficient resources to pay for essential health or nursing services and to ensure that all elderly are guaranteed necessary care.

2) Medical care for the elderly must be high quality. Health care rationing through waiting lists or the denial of services should be rejected.

3) Health care costs must be contained by increased competition of health services through expanded consumer choice and control and increased market incentives for consumers and providers of medical care. . . .

The Private Sector

The private sector can assume a greater and more responsive role in developing and marketing a more comprehensive mix of health care, social, and housing services in order to maximize opportunities in a growing elder health care marketplace. Private insurance incentives coupled with greater flexibility and creativity in public program requirements, lessons which can be learned from several international models, can hasten a more effective and efficient long-term-care delivery system—one that can truly provide the elderly with adequate protection from catastrophic and chronic illness.

Tom Jazwiecki, *Caring for an Aging World*, 1989.

Medicare provides little coverage for long-term care either in a nursing home or in the patient's own home. Yet nursing home care can be extremely costly, averaging around $2,000 per month for a resident. In the case of home health care, Medicare covers true medical care provided in the home, but it does not cover personal services such as cooking, housecleaning, dressing, feeding, and bathing.

Government should pay for the essential long-term care expenses of those Americans who do not have the resources to meet this cost or who cannot pay for it without great hardship. This will ensure that all those who need long-term care will be able to obtain it, and it will end the financial fears of those with modest incomes.

Federal and state governments currently spend over $20 billion per year for nursing home care, primarily through Medicaid. A retiree receiving Medicaid nursing home assistance is expected to contribute his or her available income and resources to the nursing home expenses, excluding a small personal needs allowance, a small amount of savings, a home of any value, a car, and other personal belongings. This is a reasonable policy, since the nursing home provides for the patient's basic needs such as food and shelter and, in the case of single patients, since no one else is dependent on the income or savings. Moreover, it is reasonable to expect Americans who can contribute to their own expenses to do so before the taxpayers are asked to pick up the bill.

Impoverished Spouses

Prior to recent legislation, the real problems with this policy occurred in cases where a nursing home patient had a healthy spouse still living in the community. In order to obtain Medicaid assistance for the spouse in a nursing home, the couple had to spend their joint income and savings on nursing home care until they were poor enough to qualify for Medicaid. As a result this policy unfairly and needlessly impoverished the noninstitution-alized spouses of nursing home patients. . . .

The next reform should be to remove this long-term care assistance from Medicaid and instead provide it through a separate program entirely dedicated to meeting the long-term care needs of the elderly poor. Medicaid was originally designed to provide basic health care services to the nonelderly poor. It was not designed to pay for long-term care for the low-income elderly, though it has been forced by circumstances to assume this responsibility. Separating these two very different functions into different programs would allow the federal and state governments to more effectively address the needs of each group.

A separate long-term care program should have more flexibility in providing long-term care services to the poor elderly. In addition to paying for nursing home care, it should also, whenever possible, pay for home care for individuals who would otherwise have to be cared for in a nursing home at much greater expense to the government. In the case of such individuals, this would mean paying part-time caregivers to help them with personal services such as cooking, cleaning, bathing, and dressing. However, for the more affluent elderly, such personal care would continue to be provided by family and friends. As part of this reform, Congress also should reevaluate the Medicare program to ensure that it offers the same coverage for genuine medical services provided in the home as it does for medical services outside the home.

The new long-term care program should be a joint federal/state enterprise, like Medicaid and most programs of assistance for the needy. Adopting the new program as described above would result in no significant increase in federal spending, but it would use existing Medicaid funds more efficiently.

If retirees lacking the funds to pay for essential long-term care services are cared for by the government, the remaining problem involves the elderly who have substantial resources but are by no means rich. The issue here is not access to needed care, which is assured, but how to protect their resources from being ravaged by high nursing home costs. It is these middle-class Americans who are most concerned about long-term care costs, since they are protected neither by great wealth nor by government aid.

A Significant Market

Private long-term-care insurance represents not just a potential financing alternative for long-term care, it represents a potentially significant product market, a market broad enough to encompass almost every segment of American society. To the elderly, private long-term-care insurance can offer an alternative to impoverishment. To middle-aged Americans, it can represent an estate- and financial-planning tool. For those younger, especially if policies are made available through employer or group sponsorship, it can represent a low-cost catastrophic insurance protection package, so essential for younger families with limited resources.

Tom Jazwiecki in *Caring for an Aging World*, 1989.

This is not really a health policy issue, however, but an estate-planning matter, which can be addressed more appropriately through private sector insurance and similar financial mechanisms. Almost by definition, such retirees have the means to pay for insurance to cover heavy long-term care costs, and they can use some of their saved resources to pay for insurance to protect the rest. The government's role should be to promote widespread use of long-term care insurance and other private financing mechanisms for those who have significant resources. The federal government should take the following specific steps to advance this policy:

Improve the data base for users. Many insurers are still reluctant to promote long-term care insurance aggressively because they lack the actuarial data needed to estimate the potential cost of claims. The federal government could undertake a thorough study, in conjunction with the insurance industry, to develop national and regional data on the degree to which the elderly at different ages use nursing homes, the length of stays, how coverage of nursing home costs affects utilization, and similar matters.

Reform the taxation of private policies. The favorable tax treatment of life insurance should be extended to long-term care insurance. This means that income earned on the investment reserves of insurance policies for long-term care would no longer be subject to tax. In addition, benefits paid by such policies would not be subject to tax.

Provide tax relief for long-term health care costs. Expenses for long-term care should be eligible for the same personal income tax credits for medical costs. That is, a 30 percent tax credit for out-of-pocket expenses and a 20 percent tax credit for premium payments for long-term care insurance. In addition, younger taxpayers would be able to receive these tax credits for money they spend on purchasing long-term care services or insurance for elderly relatives. They would be able to do this without having to meet the dependent support test, which now requires them to provide 50 percent or more of a relative's total support before they can claim the relative as a dependent and receive credits or deductions for his or her health care expenses. This would provide much needed relief to those American families facing high nursing home or home care bills.

Include long-term care insurance in "cafeteria" plans. . . . Federal tax law should be changed to allow employers to offer long-term care insurance as one choice under cafeteria employee benefit plans. These are fringe benefit plans where each worker is allowed to choose from a range of offered options those benefits that best suit his needs and preferences. Current law does not allow long-term insurance to be included as a benefit that employers can offer in such tax-free cafeteria plans.

Using Tax Deductions

Reverse DEFRA restrictions. Under the Deficit Reduction Act of 1983 (DEFRA), Congress eliminated most tax deductions and exemptions for the money contributed by employers to retirement medical benefit plans and the money earned by investing the reserve funds of those plans, including plans which provide long-term care coverage. Without such deductions and exemptions, private employers are far less inclined to provide long-term care benefits. In the absence of more comprehensive health care tax reform, this tax policy should be reversed. Employers should be allowed full deductions and exemptions for contributions and returns to reserves for employee retirement health benefit plans that include long-term care benefits, just as employers are allowed deductions and exemptions for contributions and returns to retirement pension reserves.

Allow Americans to use their retirement funds to purchase long-term care insurance. Workers and retirees should be allowed to use funds in pension plans, 401(K) plans, Individual Retirement Accounts (IRAs), and other retirement plans to make tax-free purchases of long-term care insurance. Similarly, employers should be allowed to use excess reserves in overfunded pension plans to fund long-term care health insurance benefits for their employees in retirement. This would provide a tax incentive for the purchase of long-term care policies.

Encourage the conversion of life insurance policies into long-term care insurance policies. Families buy life insurance to protect themselves against the loss of earning capacity during working years. Such protection generally is not needed to the same extent in retirement, when income usually is no longer dependent on the employment of the head of household. With high nursing home costs posing a far greater danger than death or the loss of the ability to work, it would make sense for life insurance companies to offer policies that gradually reduce the benefits payable at death and phase in benefits payable for long-term care. While there are no restrictions on such conversions under current law, insurers are not inclined to offer such policies because of insufficient demand. The government should encourage Americans to request such convertible life insurance policies by publicizing the concept. . . .

A New Approach

The elderly face real and mounting health care problems in the form of rapidly rising health costs, inadequate coverage for important health services, and a collapsing Medicare financing system that is undermining the quality of their care and imposing a growing taxation burden. These problems cannot be resolved by a further extension of the failed social insurance approach. Indeed, such an extension would only make these problems worse.

A completely new approach is needed. It must be based on competition, market incentives, and consumer choice.

"What I considered a 'last resort,' I now regard as the best decision I could have made."

Nursing Homes Are Beneficial

Lou L. Hartney

Lou L. Hartney is a free-lance writer in Montrose, Colorado. In the following viewpoint, Hartney describes her traumatic decision to place her elderly mother in a nursing home after years of caring for her at home. Guilt-ridden and uncertain at first, Hartney came to believe that placing her mother in a nursing home was positive. Hartney's mother enjoyed the companionship and structured activities the home provided.

As you read, consider the following questions:

1. What circumstances caused the author to settle her mother in a nursing home?
2. What negative reactions did Hartney's mother have to the nursing home?
3. According to Hartney, how did the nursing home help her mother?

Lou L. Hartney, "My Mother's Keeper," *The Family Therapy Networker*, September/October 1989. Reprinted with permission.

July 28, 1987: It is too late to turn back. I have set in motion events that are tumbling me along like a broken branch in flood-tide. I have run out of choices. I look at my 94-year-old mother. Her thin, hunched body is dwarfed amid a welter of crates, cartons of books, piles of possessions to go to the Salvation Army, and other stacks of worthless items too precious to leave behind. Her expression matches the disheveled room. She doesn't know it yet, but by this time next week, she will be in a nursing home in Colorado, a thousand miles from here, whatever life remains to her drastically changed. The cost of dying, particularly if one does it slowly, is prohibitive in California.

Growing Older

She is leaving kind neighbors who remember spirited bridge games in which she held her own. She now forgets their names and faces from one day to the next, but I will never stop being grateful to them for coming in to see her often in recent years, telling her over and over who they are, for including her in dinner invitations, even though they know the diapers she now wears don't always do all they are supposed to. Will we ever find people who will brighten her life like that again?

My God, what am I doing to her?

July 30, 1987: Although I feel drained and exhausted, sleep evades me for hours these nights. While I am turning endlessly, I find myself wishing she could go peacefully in her sleep before I have to do this. She is almost a stranger now, consumed by fear that I will leave her sight to go even as far as the washer in the garage. She watches anxiously from the doorway when I go to the mailbox. If I have a sitter come in when I shop for groceries, she is anxious and hurt; if I take her with me, I am frantic.

Parents in Nursing Homes

I recall her words a few years back about a lifelong friend whose son put her in a nursing home where she eventually died. "I could have told her that daughters are closer to their mothers," she said, as if that were her personal guarantee against such a thing happening to her.

Sleep, when it comes at last, is as filled with foreboding as my waking hours.

August 4, 1987: Nothing is going right. I am sick with fear. The house is sold. The new owners are moving in tomorrow. I expect to hear the sound of the moving van grinding to a stop in front of the house at any moment.

I try to reconstruct the reasoning that led me into this morass. In retrospect, it doesn't make any sense at all. I look at earlier journal entries: "I don't care about golden streets—what I want out of Heaven is not to have to clean the bathroom a dozen times a day!" and "When will I get time to work at my writing—if that day ever comes, there won't be an original thought left in my head." There are other entries made in anger that I'm ashamed to re-read. The most civilized comment I find is: "It's not her fault or mine that the 'golden years' are tarnished for us both."

The Essentials of Care

Suddenly, the former 10-hour days in my home office seem to be a haven of safety and security. Work deadlines allowed little time for worry, a blessing that had gone unrecognized until now. True, they also permitted time for only the essentials of care for my mother. I fixed her meals, kept her clean, somehow got my work out on time, had crashing headaches.

Am I ready to trade that for a burden of guilt?

August 6, 1987: It is done, or at least begun. Our flight to Colorado was not as difficult as I had feared. Friends are driving my car from California, so my daughter, Linda, who lives in the Colorado town we are going to meets us and takes us to a motel. Mom can't negotiate the stairs at Linda's home, and I can't bear to take her to the nursing home at the end of an exhausting day for her. She sleeps soundly. After breakfast at a nearby coffee shop this morning, I know the time has come to try to explain what is ahead. I force the words out, that I can no longer take care of her, that she will be living at a place called a "care center," that I will see her every day, that I love her as much as ever. "Can you understand?" I ask. Her answer is a qualified, "I'll try."

Humane Care

Much is written about inappropriate nursing home use, but policy should also consider *appropriate* nursing home use. Ironically, the greatest support to family caregivers in some case might be the provision of high-quality, humane institutional programs so that families could stop giving care—without guilt—when their (direct) help outlives its humane purpose.

Rosalie Kane, quoted in *America*, January 31, 1987.

I am expecting tears, pleas, perhaps anger, but she is outwardly calm. I wonder if she realizes what I am saying, and by the time my daughter arrives to take us to the nursing home, my face is streaked with tears. Linda puts on a cheerful front, and I wonder how I could get through it without her.

An Inspection Trip

The administrator of the nursing home, Mary, comes out to the car and greets Mom with a cheery, "Hello, Emily!" I had met Mary on an inspection trip months earlier and had been impressed by her obvious understanding and honesty. Some of the other nearby

192

facilities we had investigated had a policy of asking family members to stay away at least three days after the patient's admission. "Let us take all the flak at first," they said. "Then, when you show up, she'll be glad to see you." I felt that three days without a familiar face would be shattering to her, so when Mary assured me I could be with her as much as I wished, I made my choice.

She is put alone in a twin-bedded room. I stay until bedtime that evening and am there early the next morning. I find her sitting on the other bed in her room, a puzzled look on her face. "What day is this?" she asks. I tell her it is Friday. Her next question is, "When are we going home?" I start to explain, but she cuts me off. "You say this is Sunday?"

September 1, 1987: She has been put in a room with 97-year-old Belle. When I walk in today, my mother points toward her new roommate in her chair by the window and says, "That old woman's as deaf as a post!" As I am trying to find the right words of apology, I realize that Belle is, indeed, extremely hard of hearing and has no notion of what has just been said.

I didn't appreciate my mother's sense of tact until it was gone.

September 15, 1987: She has been in the nursing home five weeks now. I am renting a house in the country, and when I walk to my car alone, I'm often dizzy with a feeling of freedom. She begs me daily to stay all night with her. I try to convince her that two people can't sleep in a single hospital bed and, besides, the people who run the care center wouldn't allow it. She brushes my answer aside with, "They wouldn't even notice!"

She has been given a short and simple haircut. I admit I'm relieved to be freed from home permanents, shampoos, and settings, but she looks like a frail elf with a too-small head.

Trying to Understand

Part of the time she thinks she's in a hotel; other days, she asks me if it's a hospital. Today, she says, "Maybe this is a nut house—maybe you put me here because I'm nuts!" But there's no anger in her voice, no hurt, no hint of feeling betrayed. I think she is simply trying to understand.

November 12, 1987: She has good days and bad days. Her disposition, as always, is sweet. But sometimes she doesn't know her great-grandchildren, and they visit frequently. She often says, "And who are these beautiful children?" Sometimes she says to me, "Is Lou coming out today?" I answer, "Mom, I'm Lou." "Oh, of course," she says.

It is snowing today, and tree branches sag under the weight. She says, "Isn't this unusual for California?"

November 27, 1987: Today is her 95th birthday. Linda, the children, and I take fried chicken, rolls, and apple pie, all her favorites, and reserve the Activities Room, a glassed-in portion of the dining area used for special occasions. Mom goes to her regular table while we are setting things up. When I go to get her, she holds onto Belle's wheelchair. "I don't want to go unless Belle comes too," she says. That's fine with us; we just hadn't thought of it in advance. The children help her open her gifts, and the occasion comes close to gaiety.

Lonely Residents

December 17, 1987: The Christmas festivities are getting me down. Various groups are singing and bringing handmade gifts for the residents at the center. I sit with Mom as the beautiful voices fill the dining area. The staff people, too, are even kinder and more cheerful than usual. I am touched by their evident sincerity. But I am on the verge of tears throughout the holiday observances, not for my mother particularly. I tell myself my grief is for the residents who are alone, without a friend or relative there. I look at the faces around us. Some eyes are empty, like the windows of abandoned houses. Some are sad; all are sober. I can sense the weight of memories in those which comprehend the season.

An Important Function

Sometimes there is tremendous guilt in committing a parent. It may be the feeling of, my mother never sent me away, I was never too much for her, but she was too much for me. . . .

Nursing homes do fulfill an important function.

Lissy F. Jarvik, quoted in *Los Angeles Times*, April 17, 1988.

A suspicion takes shape in my mind. Is this season so hard for me because when I look into the faces near me, I see myself and my future? Can it be that, after all, my deepest fears are for myself?

Why can't we all make a choice, while awareness is still with us, as to whether or not we want to live this sort of sad half-life?

January 11, 1988: I have horrible dreams almost nightly: my mother dying in agony, a grandchild disappearing, myself buried in sliding sand, unable to cry out for help from people nearby. I wake up drenched in perspiration, shaking, crying. Breakfast is little comfort. Food, with rare exceptions, is tasteless, difficult to swallow. I walk from room to room, but the view from every window is bleak and hostile. The trees are gaunt, naked caricatures of their summer selves. Close to panic, I telephone a close friend in California who is a therapist.

"Genie," I say, "Why am I so miserable? Mom is being taken care of, I have time to myself—too much, it seems. I feel paralyzed.

194

I sit for hours and stare at the most stupid television programs. . . ."

"I'm not surprised," she says. "You're suffering from loss of purpose and feeling isolated. You miss your friends and the familiarity of your life here." She is a successful writer and knows I share her interest. After reassuring me that I'm not losing my mind, she gives me an assignment to write one page a day on any subject and send her a copy of my first week's output. "Don't worry about good writing. Just be honest. If it's nothing more than a diatribe against ice and snow, that's okay."

I hang up, feeling a little encouraged.

Companionship

February 2, 1988: My mother and Belle help fold laundry with other residents in the dining area. Staff people compliment them all on the job they do. It isn't bridge, but it's companionship.

Belle tells me she and Mom have been friends since they were young girls. I don't correct her.

Sometimes, I eat a meal with them, but today I leave for a dental appointment just as they are sitting down to wait for their lunch trays. I glance back as I reach the door of the dining hall. My mother has put her head down on the table on her folded arms. Weariness? Sadness? I wish I knew.

May 8, 1988: It's Mother's Day, and one of Belle's daughters and I plan to make a two-family party of it in the Activity Room. Several of Belle's seven living children are there. She is near the head of the table; Mom and I are at the other end. One of the daughters has brought fresh yeast rolls, homemade peach preserves, and real butter; the kitchen has prepared a feast of turkey and trimmings.

Belle is confused by all the visitors. Like Mom, she is rarely sure who's who. Also, her sight is not much better than her hearing. She strains to see the far end of the table. "Who's that?" she asks over and over, pointing toward my mother. "That's Emily, your roommate," Belle's daughter, Jane, tells her each time. By the time Belle asks again, we are all in high spirits, and Jane answers, "Oh, that's just another one of your kids, Mom." I am amazed when my mother answers, "Yes, I'm the youngest one!" It nearly breaks up the party. I never think of asking for a miracle, but this is one. My mother has not been intentionally humorous in years. . . .

July 21, 1988: I have come to a decision which surprises me: I think my mother is actually happier here than she was at home with me. There, she lay on the sofa most of the day while I sat at my word processor, my earphones making even casual conversation impossible. Now, she is never bored. There are aides in and out of the room all day. Her excursions down the hall to be lifted into and out of her bath by a hydraulic contraption are small adventures. There are exercise classes in which residents sit in a circle and move whatever still answers the command, mostly arms, of course. Various clergymen rotate Sunday services. All holidays are observed with decorations and activities. There is even one called "Harvest Day" with prizewinning vegetables displayed on bales of hay out in front and a hayride in a horse-drawn wagon for those able to manage it. With so many companions of similar age, she is free of the "last leaf on the tree" syndrome.

There is also a weekly class on Colorado history, which I attend with her one day and find fascinating. Mom pays little attention, but she smiles at me a lot and pats my hand constantly. And twice a week, a mental health professional gathers certain residents, Mom and Belle among them, in the Activity Room. I don't feel that I should ask to listen in, but I understand the purpose is to help maintain stability for those who are in greatest danger of slipping away from reality. I wait at the door today for them to come out. On the way back to the room, I say, "What do you talk about in your meeting?" "I'm not sure," she answers and leans down over the chair she is pushing to shout to Belle, "What did we talk about today?" "Oh, not much of anything," is Belle's answer. Still, I sense a feeling of importance in both of them at having been singled out for special attention.

No Longer Feeling Guilty

August 2, 1988: On my way to see her today, I feel strangely lighthearted. I have cut my visits back to every other day, talking to her several times on the telephone on alternate days. I'm living life on a level new to me, walking down country roads as the day comes to life, writing, swimming, and trying to capture on film sky and clouds seen through an old barbed wire fence. Best of all, I'm no longer feeling guilty. What I considered a "last resort," I now regard as the best decision I could have made. I don't mean that it's nirvana, but both of us are several steps closer than we were before.

When I walk into the room today, she is glad to see me. She asks me several times if it's Sunday. I say, "No, Mom, it's Tuesday." She rolls Belle's wheelchair up close to where I am sitting. I read letters from relatives to her, and she seems to listen attentively. I am not prepared for her comment out of the blue while I am putting the letters back into their envelopes. "I like my life," she says. I sit, stunned, wondering if mental telepathy is operating between us. I start to tell her how happy her words make me, but the moment is gone. She pats my hand and asks again, "You say this is Sunday?"

"The average nursing home promotes passivity and immobility which can and do lead to total disability."

Nursing Homes Are Harmful

Nancy Fox

In the following viewpoint, Nancy Fox argues that nursing homes are harmful to the elderly. The staffs of nursing homes, the author asserts, hurt elderly patients by treating them like children, neglecting them, and ignoring their true needs. Fox is a nurse and an author specializing in issues relating to the elderly.

As you read, consider the following questions:

1. Why do some nursing home staff members mistreat elderly patients, according to the author?
2. What measures does the author advocate to counteract the harm that nursing homes cause?
3. According to Fox, how can harm to the elderly in nursing homes be prevented?

"Cutie, it's time to go potty-chair!"

"Are we ready for our little pill, Ducky?"

"Here, let's put on our bib, shall we?"

These comments are samples of "infantizing," that is, the pressuring of an institutionalized adult into a state of infancy. This is the first of three practices that robs him of identity, of self-esteem and contributes to mental decline. It induces what I call "man-made senility."

While only a small percentage of the elderly suffer incurable irreversible brain damage (including those nearly two million diagnosed with Alzheimer's disease), countless others fall prey to preventable, reversible confusion of mind. Torsos tilting sideways, eyes glassy, mouths drooling—do you think that in old age these symptoms are inevitable?

Long Term Care

In a federal study on long term care, surveyors noted that in many facilities, patients' dependency attitudes were constantly reinforced by the manner in which staff addressed them, often as though speaking to a child. Mrs. Amy Park can tell you about "infantizing."

A dress protector is tied around her neck, only they call it a "bib." She keeps hearing words like "diapers," "honey-child," and wonders when they will hand her a rattle or chuck her under the chin with a giggly "goo-goo-ga-ga!" Simply because of diminished sight and poor health, she has been stripped of her adult status, molded into a miniature of her former self.

"Treat me like a child, call me 'Cutie,'" exclaims her roommate, "and I will stamp my feet and throw my food on the floor. But then, you can't win. People will call me 'senile.'"

Across the hall Mr. Pruitt tosses in the night. He longs for a glass of warm milk but this time he won't ring his call bell. He can't forget the response he got the last time. Said the nursing assistant: "If we'd eaten our din-din last night we wouldn't be so hungry now, would we?"

But Mr. McGuire tackles the "opposition" head-on. Into his room trips the new little aide. "Are we ready for our bath?" she squeals. "YES," bellows the disgusted old gentleman, "*WE* are ready. *Let's* jump in!"

Instant Diagnosis

Sick of being babied, Mr. Hardy's tactics for resistance are slightly irregular. On his bed he lies stark naked. Every morning you can count on it—covers, pajamas piled on the floor. Staff walks in, scowls, walks out. Mr. Hardy smirks. "That'll fix 'em!" Considering themselves experts at instant diagnosis, employees label him "senile, childish, dirty-old man." For our strip-teaser it's the old "shame-on-you, you-naughty-naughty-boy" approach. Staff is old: "Other than provide food and medications, just ignore him."

Granted this man's behavior is difficult. But to one nurse he seems alert, reasonably intelligent, certainly not "senile." Is he lonely, she wonders? Is he protesting our condescending approach? Then perhaps he needs more, rather than less attention. Proceeding on this premise, she enters his room, pulls up the covers and says: "Mr. Hardy, I see by your chart that you hail from the great state of Texas?"

No response. Mr. Hardy turns to the wall. "And that before retirement you taught biology?"

"Big deal. What do you care? Drop dead!"

Each day this nurse repeats the procedure, varying her questions and conversation. Finally, though suspicious of her sincerity, Mr. Hardy reacts. He begins to talk. He moans of his past failures, of his children who never visit, of his divorce. Here, masked by melodramatics, is a thinking, feeling human being, starved for meaningful relationships.

In time, aides enter his room to find him fully dressed, talking with his roommate. Staff learns to accept and appreciate him. They bring him science books from the library and track down a fellow biologist from the local high school who becomes a regular visitor. In return, Mr. Hardy reads to bedfast patients, waters plants, pushes wheelchairs. Formerly afraid of him, staff now may be seen, their arms around him, walking together down the hall.

The Ongoing Problem of Abuse

Although there *are* some "good" nursing homes which seek to put purpose in the lives of their clients, the problem of abuse runs rampant. So you thought abuse was snuffed out when, in the 1960s those scandals were exposed? So you believed that when the phrase "Nursing Home" was scrapped in favor of "Health Care Centers," the problems were licked? So you thought indignities ceased to exist when citizen action groups demanded reforms? Well, I have news for you. One cannot legislate caring. And although things look better today; although the worst abuses are found in a limited number of homes, very few facilities get off scot-free.

Nancy Fox, *The Patient Comes First*, 1988.

In despair, Mr. Hardy had uncovered his body. But when the staff uncovered his heart and mind; when they conversed with him adult-to-adult, they discovered the real Mr. Hardy, the man he had always been, a human being of dignity and worth.

The second contributor to "man-made senility" is called, quite simply, "rest."

"Rest?" you exclaim. "Come now. What's wrong with rest? We all need it."

Would you believe that rest, this seemingly harmless pastime, can demoralize a person if taken in too large doses? It's that "you-need-your-rest" syndrome, sanctioned by too many "rest" homes. Too much—no end of rest.

Gerontologists generally agree that one of the most dangerous treatments for the elderly is enforced inactivity. (This applies, in fact, to persons of any age.) Yet the average nursing home promotes passivity and immobility which can and do lead to total disability.

"Nonsense," you protest, "they have activity programs galore—the law requires it."

Yes, but take a count. What percentage of clients actually participate in activities at all? And how many do this on a daily basis? How many residents sit in the halls for hours on end, staring at walls?

"Nonsense again," you insist. "Nobody ever died of rest."

Oh no? If he could, the late Mr. Carr would disagree with you. What happened to him happens to far too many shut-ins. Arriving at the home, he is introduced to his roommate and to the staff. After that, not much communication, for repeatedly he is told: "Time to rest. Doctor's orders." And so he gets it. Plenty of rest. Mornings he lolls in his bed. Afternoons he dozes in his chair. Evenings, he's put to bed at a child's early hour. After only one week, Mr. Carr begins to see for himself a bleak future.

Lack of Stimulation

Months pass. Lack of physical and mental stimulation take their toll. His interest in life drained, Mr. Carr now qualifies for the "Seniles Club." He forgets easily. Mumbles to himself. Bladder and sphincter control gone, he soils himself, gets frequently scolded. Time now to join that catheterized, bed-ridden, faceless throng, victims of the "plenty-of-rest" school of thought. Soon he develops a bladder infection, then bedsores. Not surprisingly, he is hospitalized for pneumonia, suffers transplantation shock. Totally confused. His latest medical orders? You guessed it. "Plenty of rest!"

"Yes," agrees the staff, "he needs his rest."

Three days later he gets the best rest there is, the most perfect rest known to "man." He's resting in peace. A sheet is pulled over his head.

Positive that they have provided tender loving care, unaware of mismanagement, the medical and nursing staffs make the standard comment: "Oh, well, Harry's better off now. Nothing to live for!"

Perhaps you, the reader, have an inkling what happens to minds and bodies when all this resting goes on, even though health professionals often forget that this can trigger:

© Germano/Rothco

Dulling of the intellect
Metabolic imbalances
Increased dependency
Circulatory deterioration
Mental confusion
Lack of sensory stimulation
Loss of muscular strength
Loss of bone calcium
Deterioration of the cerebro-vascular system and finally,
Loss of self-esteem and will to live.

Although today many physicians and nurses are cutting down on those interminable rest periods, they are often opposed by other staff members or relatives of the patient who complain: "Why change his routine? Old people have worked hard all their lives—they deserve their rest!"

Dangerous Tranquility

The third contributor to "man-made senility" is a drug—that medically prescribed tranquilizer.

The next time you visit a nursing home, extend your antennae. With eyes, ears, and nose, tune in—don't just observe, *scrutinize* the place. Peek into remote corners. Take the elevator to the top floors where certain "hopeless" patients may be stashed away, out of sight, out of the public mind. In some homes, especially in large cities, what do you find? Patients not recognizing their families. Heads flopping into supper trays. Bodies tied to chairs. Voices mumbling, cackling, wailing, screaming. Of course, ravaging diseases such as advanced Alzheimer's can cause these conditions. But, barring those, our immediate concern is: How many of these unfortunates are paying the penalty of months, even years of mismanagement? How many were "infantized," over-rested, over-sedated? We ask the burning question: *"Is this senility necessary?"*

According to one estimate, over one hundred million dollars worth of tranquilizers are used yearly in U.S. nursing homes. They put people in a position where they won't complain or expect service. And it's a fine way to hasten "senility."

Jails are filled with political prisoners. Many of our elders, too, living in jails of their own, are prisoners of altered states of consciousness. Says Dr. Alexander Simon (for years the medical director of Langley-Porter Neuro-Psychiatric Institute in San Francisco): "Once you start giving any kind of sedative medication that has an effect on the metabolism of the brain, you may precipitate an acute confusional state, especially likely in aged patients. This can easily be mistaken for senility."

For every drug consumed, there are side effects. Each new one added increases the potential for reaction. And so, what about *reactions* which are treated by adding *more* drugs? Consider this ad, placed in professional journals: "If drug-induced Parkinsonism threatens to interrupt tranquilizer therapy, just add—(drug name withheld)." A pyramid. One drug atop another ad infinitum. . . .

Patients' Rights

Another thought. What about the legality of overdrugging? Excessive use of tranquilizers may infringe on patients' rights.

These, then, are three contributors to "man-made senility." Infantizing, over rest and overdrugging. Torsos tilting sideways, eyes glassy, mouths drooling—*no!* In late life, these are not inevitable.

According to Dr. Mary Wolanin (voted the 1982 Gerontological Nurse of the Year) there are a hundred physiological causes of mental confusion which are reversible or preventable. (Not to mention the many psychological causes.) Some examples: Anemia, stress, drugs, constipation, poor nutrition, hearing loss, transplantation shock, hypertension.

If your loved one seems to be suffering from one or many of these reversible conditions, need you stand by helpless? It is your legal and human right to investigate. Question the doctor and nursing staff. What else can you do?

Observe staff attitudes. Do they talk down or do they speak "adult-to-adult" to your relative? Monitor the amount of rest or inactivity in an average week. Is the patient receiving any kind of therapy? Why not? This is a "*Health Care* Center" isn't it? It's *not* a hotel!

Finally, obtain information. Exactly what drugs is your relative taking, for how long and for what purpose? Are these drugs for his benefit or for staff convenience? Watch him closely. Is he changing, improving, sliding downhill? Losing ground mentally and physically?

Centers for Living

My hope is that you and your relative are satisfied with the staff and administration and with the overall care and pleasant conditions. Tell them so. If this is truly a "Center for Living," give credit where it is due. Those of you who have watched the nursing home evolve from what it was twenty years ago have seen gratifying changes, even in the area of tranquilizers. There's still a long way to go. No longer will the public tolerate that "wring-out-the-old" approach wherever it is still found. No longer should any of us stand for preventable "man-made senility" wherever that is found. Speak up if you must. If you are worried, confront the powers that be, that they take a closer look at the condition of your relative. Ask them outright:

"Is this senility necessary?"

a critical thinking activity

Evaluating Sources of Information

A critical thinker must always question sources of information. Historians, for example, distinguish between *primary sources* (eyewitness accounts, documents, or artifacts) and *secondary sources* (writings or statements based on primary sources or other secondary sources). The story of a seventy-year-old woman, who describes the conditions provided at her nursing home, is an example of a primary source. The account of a reporter who interviewed the elderly woman is an example of a secondary source.

Interpretation and/or point of view also play a role when dealing with both primary and secondary sources. An elderly woman with a serious health problem who needed a great deal of care may evaluate the same nursing home differently than a healthy elderly woman would. It is up to the researcher to keep in mind the potential biases of his or her sources.

Test your skill in evaluating sources of information by completing the following exercise. Imagine you are writing a report on what type of long-term health care would be best for the elderly. Listed below are a number of sources which may be useful for your research. *Place a P next to those descriptions you believe are primary sources.* Second, *rank the primary sources assigning the number (1) to what appears to be the most accurate and fair primary source, the number (2) to the next most accurate, and so on until the ranking is finished.* Next, *place an S next to those descriptions you believe are secondary sources and rank them also, using the same criteria.*

If you are doing this activity as a member of a class or group, discuss and compare your evaluation with other members of the group. Others may come to different conclusions than you. Listening to their reasons may give you valuable insights in evaluating sources of information.

P = primary
S = secondary

204

_____ 1. The diary of an elderly man who lived in a nursing home for ten years. _____

_____ 2. A book entitled *America's Youth: The Neglected Resource*, which contends the government spends too little on children and too much on the elderly. _____

_____ 3. An interview with a woman who works for the American Association of Retired Persons. The woman contends that most nursing homes abuse their patients. _____

_____ 4. An article in *Time* magazine analyzing the benefits of hospice care for infirm elderly patients. _____

_____ 5. A video on home care for the elderly. _____

_____ 6. A lecture given by an economics professor who argues that national health insurance for the elderly would bankrupt the government. _____

_____ 7. A speech given by Senator Edward M. Kennedy on the necessity of government-financed, long-term home care. _____

_____ 8. A television documentary on the care of the elderly in nursing homes. _____

_____ 9. A comentary written by a geriatrician for the *Journal of the American Medical Association*, which advocates that social insurance pay the elderly's medical costs. _____

_____ 10. A federal study conducted by the Administration on Aging on the drawbacks of using Medicare to pay for long-term health care. _____

_____ 11. Pamphlets produced by the organization Americans for Generational Equity which oppose government funding for health care programs for the elderly. _____

Periodical Bibliography

The following articles have been selected to supplement the diverse views presented in this chapter.

Richard Besdine	"The Maturing of Geriatrics," *The New England Journal of Medicine*, January 19, 1989.
Susan Dentzer	"The Next Big Ticket: Long-Term Health Care," *U.S. News & World Report*, August 8, 1988.
John Elson	"Rationing Medical Care," *Time*, May 15, 1989.
Peter Fuhrman	"Go Home and Die," *Forbes*, May 16, 1988.
Michael Gartner	"The 'Golden Years' and Medicine: An Age-Old Challenge," *The Wall Street Journal*, April 7, 1988.
Clyde A. Hanks	"Before the Well Runs Dry: Cutting the Cost of Retiree Health Benefits," *USA Today*, May 1989.
Anne Harvey	"Life-Care Contracts for the Elderly: A Risky Retirement," *USA Today*, July 1988.
Laurence B. McCullough	"Long-Term Care: Policy, Ethics, and Advocacy," *Hastings Center Report*, September/October 1989.
Michael D. Reagan	"Health Care Rationing: What Does It Mean," *The New England Journal of Medicine*, October 27, 1988.
Robert J. Samuelson	"The Cost of Chaos," *Newsweek*, October 2, 1989.
Harry Schwartz	"The Right Medicine," *National Review*, March 10, 1989.
Leonard Sloane	"When Health Care Comes to the Home," *The New York Times*, January 28, 1989.
Louis W. Sullivan	"The Health Care Priorities of the Bush Administration," *The New England Journal of Medicine*, July 13, 1989.
Stephen P. Wallace and Carroll L. Estes	"Health Policy for the Elderly," *Society*, September/October 1989.

Organizations To Contact

The editors have compiled the following list of organizations which are concerned with the issues debated in this book. All of them have information or publications available for interested readers. The descriptions are derived from materials provided by the organizations. This list was compiled upon the date of publication. Names and phone numbers of organizations are subject to change.

American Association of Homes for the Aging (AAHA)
1129 20th St. NW, Suite 400
Washington, DC 20036
(202) 828-9432

AAHA is a national trade organization that represents not-for-profit nursing homes, retirement communities, senior housing facilities and community service agencies. The Association strives to provide housing designed to meet the specific needs of each elderly American. It has published *Partnership in Creating Communities That Care: Meeting the Housing Needs of Older Americans, Reforming Care for the Aged and Disabled: Who Cares, Who Plans, Who Pays?, The American Public Views on Long-Term Care*, as well as a publications catalog listing other available materials.

American Association of Retired Persons (AARP)
1909 K St. NW
Washington, DC 20049
(202) 872-4700

AARP is one of the most influential senior citizen lobbying organizations in the country. AARP advocates expanding Social Security benefits, increasing government funding for the elderly's health care, and ending discrimination against the elderly. Its Legal Counsel for the Elderly center provides legal services to people sixty years and older. AARP publishes *AARP News Bulletin*, the bimonthly magazine *Modern Maturity*, as well as other publications.

The American College of Health Care Administrators (ACHCA)
325 S. Patrick St.
Alexandria, VA 22314
(703) 549-5822

The College's members are health care and nursing home administrators. ACHCA encourages research in all aspects of geriatrics and maintains a library on health care and long-term care administration. It publishes *Long-Term Care Administrator* monthly and also publishes educational materials.

American Enterprise Institute for Public Policy Research (AEI)
1150 17th St. NW
Washington, DC 20036
(202) 862-5800

AEI is a conservative research and educational association that provides information to professionals and the public on national and international public policy issues. AEI has a library and has published materials on health care for the elderly and on Social Security. AEI publishes the bimonthly *Public Opinion* and *Regulation*.

The American Geriatrics Society (AGS)
770 Lexington Ave., Suite 400
New York, NY 10021
(212) 308-1414

AGS comprises physicians who are interested in the problems of the elderly. The Society encourages and promotes the study of geriatrics and emphasizes the importance of medical research in the field of aging. It publishes the monthly *Clinical Report on Aging*, the monthly *Journal*, and other publications.

American Medical Association (AMA)
535 N. Dearborn St.
Chicago, IL 60610
(312) 645-5000

The AMA is the nation's largest organization of health care professionals. It advocates increasing government funding for health care for the elderly and often represents the medical profession before Congress and governmental agencies. The AMA advocates stricter enforcement of the laws protecting the elderly from abuse and supports home health care. The Association produces the weekly *American Medical News* and *Journal of the American Medical Association* and numerous other medicine-oriented materials.

Americans for Generational Equity (AGE)
608 Massachusetts Ave. NE, First Floor
Washington, DC 20002
(202) 546-3131

AGE believes too much of the government's resources are going to the elderly and that this misallocation of resources jeopardizes the future of America's young people. It publishes the monthly *Newsletter* and the *Age Answerman* booklet.

Cato Institute
224 Second St. SE
Washington, DC 20003
(202) 546-0200

The Cato Institute is dedicated to expanding the social and economic freedoms of the capitalist system. It opposes government funding of health care and advocates reforming Social Security. The Institute publishes the monthly *Policy Report* and the *Cato Journal*.

Coalition of Advocates for the Rights of the Infirm Elderly (CARIE)
1315 Walnut St., Suite 900
Philadelphia, PA 19107
(215) 545-5728

CARIE aids the infirm elderly and those who provide care for them. The Coalition provides community education and outreach, legislative and regulatory monitoring, and a task force that recommends solutions to elder abuse. It maintains CARIE LINE, a telephone referral service that provides information on topics dealing with the welfare of the elderly. The Coalition publishes an occasional newsletter and provides an information packet on request.

Families United for Senior Action Foundation (Families USA Foundation)
1334 G St. NW
Washington, DC 20005
(202) 628-3030

The Families USA Foundation is a national organization that focuses on improving living conditions for low-income senior citizens, families, and minorities. The Foundation believes the government should increase spending on the elderly through expanding the Supplemental Security Income program, food stamps, and federally assisted housing. It opposes cutbacks in Medicare coverage. The Foundation publishes a program policy statement and a multi-year report. The Families USA Foundation was formerly called The Villers Foundation.

Gray Panthers Project Fund, Inc.
311 S. Juniper St., Suite 601
Philadelphia, PA 19107
(215) 545-6555

Founded by Maggie Kuhn in 1970, the Gray Panthers have vociferously defended the elderly's rights. They support the creation of a national health system, safe, affordable housing, and the protection of Social Security. They are against forced retirement at age 65 and any cuts in funds for Medicare and Medicaid. The Gray Panthers organize demonstrations to support their causes and conduct seminars and research on age-related issues. Their publications include the quarterly newspaper *Network*, the bimonthly newsletter *Health Watch*, *Gray Panther Media Watch Guide*, an "Ageism" packet, and a "Campaign for a National Health Program" packet.

The Hastings Center
360 Broadway
Hastings-on-Hudson, NY 10706
(914) 762-8500

The members of The Hastings Center research moral issues created by advances in modern medicine and technology. The Center studies aging, care of the dying, nursing homes, and long-term care. The Hastings Center has published *In Search of Equity*, *Ethical Challenges of Chronic Illness*, and the bimonthly *Hastings Center Report*.

The Heritage Foundation
214 Massachusetts Ave. NE
Washington, DC 20002
(202) 546-4400

The Foundation is a conservative public policy research institute. It believes reducing government spending on Social Security and Medicare could reduce the federal budget deficit. In addition to hundreds of books and papers, the Foundation publishes a quarterly journal, *Policy Review*, the periodic *Backgrounder*, and the *Heritage Lectures* series.

Institute for Contemporary Studies (ICS)
243 Kearny St.
San Francisco, CA 94108
(415) 981-5353

ICS has published materials which argue that the Social Security system is financially unsound and must be reformed. Other publications have maintained that the U.S. allocates too much of its resources to the elderly and too few to the young. The Institute has published *World Crisis in Social Security*, *On Borrowed Time: How the Growth in Entitlement Spending Threatens America's Future*, among other books. It also publishes *The Letter* three times a year.

National Health Information Center
PO Box 1133
Washington, DC 20013
(703) 522-2590

With a database of 1100 organizations, the Center assists consumers and health-care workers in finding health information by referring them to appropriate sources. It publishes *Healthfinder*, and a series of books including *Financing Personal Health Care, Medications,* and *Vitamins.*

National Institute on Aging (NIA)
Public Information Office
Federal Building, Room 6C12
9000 Rockville Pike
Bethesda, MD 20892
(301) 496-1752

NIA is part of the National Institutes of Health. It is the federal government's prin-cipal agency for conducting and supporting biomedical, social, and behavioral research related to the aging process. The Institute gathers information from studies on elderly people, particularly on new methods of diagnosing and treating Alzheimer's disease. The Public Information Office publishes the fact sheets *Health Resources for Older Women, Answers About Aging,* and *Age Pages.* A list of materials is available on request.

National Senior Citizens Law Center
2025 M St. NW, Suite 400
Washington, DC 20036
(202) 887-5280

The Center provides legal assistance for the elderly poor. The Center publishes and distributes manuals and periodicals dealing with the legal problems of the elderly poor. It publishes the newsletter *Washington Weekly,* and the monthly *Nursing Home Law Letter.*

Public Agenda Foundation (PAF)
Six E. 39th St., Ninth Floor
New York, NY 10016
(212) 686-6610

PAF is a public policy research group that publishes information advocating the reduction of federal spending on health care and social welfare. The Foundation produces reports and pamphlets and conducts citizen education campaigns such as HealthVote, SchoolVote, and public summits. It publishes the booklets, *Putting the Work Ethic to Work, Health Care for the Elderly: Moral Dilemmas, Mortal Choices, Curbing Health Care Costs: The Public's Prescription, The Public Debt, Options for Social Welfare Policy: The Public's Views,* and *The Public's Perspective on Social Welfare Reform.*

Save Our Security (SOS)
Coalition to Protect Social Security
1201 16th St. NW, Suite 222
Washington, DC 20036
(202) 822-7848

SOS is a coalition of over 100 national, state, and local labor, aging, and disability groups established to protect and improve Social Security. It lobbies against benefit cuts. It favors expanding the Supplemental Security Income program. The SOS Education Fund conducts research, education programs, public conferences, and forums. SOS publishes *Cutting Social Security Benefits Is Unnecessary and Wrong, Social Security: A Sound and Durable System, Modified Earnings Sharing as an Approach,* and the periodic newsletter *The Bulletin.*

Bibliography of Books

Henry J. Aaron,
Barry P. Bosworth, and
Gary T. Burtless

Can America Afford to Grow Old?: Paying for Social Security. Washington, DC: The Brookings Institution, 1989.

W. Andrew Achenbaum

Social Security: Visions and Revisions. New York: Cambridge University Press, 1986.

Jo Alexander, Debbie
Berrow, Lisa Domitrovich,
Margarita Donnelly, and
Chery McLean

Women and Aging: An Anthology by Women. Corvallis, OR: Calyx Press, 1987.

Phillip Berman

The Courage to Grow Old. New York: Ballantine Books, 1989.

Robert H. Blank

Rationing Medicine. New York: Columbia University Press, 1988.

Joan M. Boyle and
James E. Morriss

The Mirror of Time: Images of Aging and Dying. New York: Greenwood Press, 1987.

Timothy H. Brubaker

Aging, Health, and Family. Beverly Hills, CA: Sage Publications, 1987.

Daniel Callahan

Setting Limits. New York: Simon & Schuster, 1987.

Larry R. Churchill

Rationing Health Care in America: Perceptions and Principles of Justice. Notre Dame, IN: University of Notre Dame Press, 1987.

William F. Clark,
Anabel O. Pelham, and
Marleen L. Clark

Old and Poor: A Critical Assessment of the Low-Income Elderly. Lexington, MA: Lexington Books, 1988.

Thomas R. Cole and
Sally A. Gadow

What Does It Mean to Grow Old? Durham, NC: Duke University Press, 1986.

Baba Copper

Over the Hill. Freedom, CA: The Crossing Press, 1988.

Norman Daniels

Am I My Parents' Keeper? New York: Oxford University Press, 1988.

Paula Brown Doress,
Diana Laskin Siegal, and
the Midlife and Older
Women Book Project

Ourselves, Growing Old: Women Aging with Knowledge and Power. New York: Simon & Schuster, 1987.

Charles J. Dougherty

American Health Care: Realities, Rights, and Reforms. New York: Oxford University Press, 1988.

Ken Dychtwald and
Joe Flower

Age Wave. Los Angeles: Jeremy P. Tarcher Inc., 1989.

Ursula A. Falk

On Our Own: Independent Living for Older Persons. Buffalo, NY: Prometheus Books, 1989.

Peter J. Ferrara

Social Security: Prospects for Real Reforms. Washington, DC: Cato Institute, 1985.

Anne Foner

Aging and Old Age: New Perspectives. Englewood Cliffs, NJ: Prentice-Hall, 1986.

Nancy Fox	*You, Your Parent, and the Nursing Home.* Buffalo, NY: Prometheus Books, 1989.
Hoyt Gimlin, ed.	*Beyond Reagan: Setting the Next Agenda.* Washington, DC: Congressional Quarterly Inc., 1987.
Christopher Hallowell	*Growing Old, Staying Young.* New York: William Morrow and Co. Inc., 1985.
Charlene Harrington et al.	*Long Term Care of the Elderly.* Beverly Hills, CA: Sage Publications, 1985.
Jo Horne	*The Nursing Home Handbook.* Washington, DC: American Association of Retired Persons, 1989.
Colleen L. Johnson and Leslie A. Grant	*The Nursing Home in American Society.* Baltimore: The Johns Hopkins University Press, 1985.
Maxwell Jones	*Growing Old, The Ultimate Freedom.* New York: Human Sciences Press, 1989.
Rosalie A. Kane and Robert L. Kane	*Long Term Care: Principles, Programs, and Politics.* New York: Springer Publishing Co., 1987.
Rosalie A. Kane and Robert L. Kane	*A Will and a Way.* New York: Columbia University Press, 1985.
James Kenny and Stephen Spicer	*Eldercare.* Buffalo, NY: Prometheus Books, 1989.
Richard D. Lamm	*Megatraumas: America at the Year 2000.* Boston: Houghton Mifflin Co., 1985.
Phillip Longman	*Born To Pay.* Boston: Houghton Mifflin Co., 1987.
Colleen McGuiness	*Aging in America: The Federal Government's Role.* Washington, DC: Congressional Quarterly Inc., 1989.
Kyriakos S. Markides and Cary L. Cooper	*Aging, Stress, and Health.* New York: John Wiley & Sons, 1989.
Charles W. Meyer	*Social Security.* Lexington, MA: Lexington Books, 1987.
Marilyn D. Petersen and Diana L. White	*Health Care of the Elderly.* Beverly Hills, CA: Sage Publications, 1989.
Alan Pifer and Lydia Bronte	*Our Aging Society: Paradox and Promise.* New York: W.W. Norton, 1986.
John W. Riley Jr. and Matilda White Riley	*The Quality of Aging: Strategies for Intervention.* Beverly Hills, CA: Sage Publications, 1989.
Alice M. Rivlin and Joshua M. Wiener	*Caring for the Disabled Elderly: Who Will Pay?* Washington, DC: The Brookings Institution, 1988.
James H. Schulz	*The Economics of Aging.* Dover, MA: Auburn House Publishing Co., 1988.
Timothy M. Smeeding et al.	*Should Medical Care Be Rationed by Age?* Totowa, NJ: Rowman & Littlefield, 1987.
Shirlynn Spacapan and Stuart Oskamp	*The Social Psychology of Aging.* Beverly Hills, CA: Sage Publications, 1989.
Stuart F. Spicker, Stanley R. Ingman, and Stan R. Lawson	*Ethical Dimensions of Geriatric Care: Value Conflicts for the 21st Century.* Norwell, CA: Kluwer Academic Publishers, 1987.

Index